Rocks & Minerals

A Field Guide to the Land of 10,000 Lakes

Dan R. Lynch & Bob Lynch

T0126030

Adventu...
Cambridge, Minnesota

Dedication

To Nancy Lynch, wife of Bob and mother of Dan, for her love and continued support of our book projects.

And to Julie Kirsch, Dan's wife, for her love and patience.

Acknowledgments

Thanks to the following for providing specimens and/or information: George Robinson, Ph.D., Phil Burgess, Robert Weikert, Bradley A. Hansen, Bruce Goetteman, Jim Cordes, Christopher Cordes, John Woerheide, Dave Woerheide, Terry Roses, Eric Powers, Dean Montour, Keith Bartel, David Gredzens, Michael P. Basal, Peter Giangrande, Jodie Blegen and Bob Wright.

Photography by Dan R. Lynch

Cover and book design by Jonathan Norberg

Edited by Brett Ortler

15 14 13 12 11 10 9 8

Minnesota Rocks & Minerals
Copyright © 2011 by Dan R. Lynch and Bob Lynch
Published by Adventure Publications
An imprint of AdventureKEEN
310 Garfield Street South
Cambridge, Minnesota 55008
(800) 678-7006
www.adventurepublications.net
All rights reserved
Printed in China
ISBN 978-1-59193-302-1 (pbk.)

Table of Contents

Introduction

Known as the "Land of 10,000 Lakes," Minnesota is more famous for its lakes than for its rocks and minerals, yet Minnesota's geology is wonderfully diverse. In fact, Minnesota has a little bit of everything, including some of the world's oldest rocks, fossils of some of the first life-forms on earth, three important iron ranges, and, of course, beautiful, collectible gems. This variety exists because of the state's complex geological history; over the past three billion years, Minnesota has undergone a series of violent volcanic events, seen the rise and fall of inland seas, and large portions of its landscape were scoured by mile-thick glaciers that later formed Minnesota's many lakes (of which there are actually 11,842). From the majestic cliffs of volcanic rock along Lake Superior's shoreline to the rolling plains of the south, Minnesota provides a stunning backdrop for your search for agates, iron minerals and fossils. This book features the most prominent, collectible and sought-after Minnesota minerals, and explains in nontechnical terms how to identify your discoveries.

Important Terms

Books about geology, rocks and minerals can be quite technical. To make this book intuitive for novices, but useful for experienced collectors, we've included important geological terms in the text, but we "translate" the phrases immediately after using them by providing a brief definition. In this way, amateurs can learn some of the more significant terms in an easy, straightforward manner. Of course, all of the geology-related terms we've used are defined in the glossary found at the back of this book as well. But for those entirely new to rock and mineral collecting, there are a few very important terms you should understand not only before you begin researching and collecting minerals, but even before you read this book.

Many people go hunting for rocks and minerals without knowing the difference between the two. The difference is simple: a **mineral** is formed from the crystallization (solidification) of a chemical compound, a combination of elements. For example, silicon dioxide, a chemical compound consisting of the elements silicon and oxygen, crystallizes to form quartz, the most abundant mineral on earth. A **rock**, on the other hand, is a mass of solid material containing a mixture of many different minerals. While pure minerals exhibit very definite and testable characteristics, such as a consistent hardness and a distinct repeating shape, rocks do not and vary greatly because of the various minerals contained within them. This can make rocks far more difficult for amateurs to identify.

A **crystal** is a solid object with a distinct shape and a repeating atomic structure created by the solidification of a chemical compound. In other words, when different elements come together, they form a chemical compound which will take on a very particular shape when it hardens. For example, the mineral galena is lead sulfide, a chemical compound consisting of lead and sulfur, which **crystallizes**, or solidifies, into the shape of a cube. A "repeating atomic structure" means that when a crystal grows, it builds upon itself. If you compared two crystals of galena, one an inch long and the other a foot long, they would have the same identical cubic shape. If a mineral is not found in a well-crystallized form but rather as a solid, rough chunk, it is said to be **massive**. If a mineral typically forms **massively**, it will frequently be found as irregular pieces or masses, rather than as well-formed crystals.

Cleavage is the property of some minerals to break in a particular way when carefully struck. As solid as minerals may seem, many have planes of weakness within them that derive from the mineral's crystal structure. These points of weakness are called **cleavage planes** and it is along these planes that some minerals will **cleave**, or separate, when struck. For example, galena has cubic cleavage, and even the most irregular piece of galena will fragment into perfect cubes if carefully broken.

Luster is the intensity with which a mineral reflects light. The luster of a mineral is described by comparing its reflectivity to that of a known material. A mineral with glassy luster, for example, is similar to the "shininess" of window glass. The distinction of a "dull" luster is reserved for the most poorly reflective minerals, while "adamantine" describes the most brilliant. But determining a mineral's luster is a subjective experience, so not all observers will necessarily agree.

Finally, one of the more specific terms used in this book is silica. **Silica** is the common name for silicon dioxide, an extremely prevalent compound that contributes to the formation of thousands of minerals. When pure silica crystallizes, it forms quartz, so it is often called the "quartz compound."

Minnesota's Geological History

Midcontinent Rift and the North Shore

Throughout the history of our planet, the land we now call North America has undergone innumerable transformations caused by geological events. By looking at rock formations found around the continent, we can decipher what those events were and when they happened. In fact one of the most significant geological events to occur in North America took place in Minnesota, and evidence of this can be found in Minnesota along Lake Superior's shore, yet most visitors don't know it.

Approximately 1.1 billion years ago, before any life existed on land, all of the earth's continents were part of a giant landmass called Rodinia. As the tectonic plates (the immense sheets of rock that underlie the earth's surface) began to shift, an enormous rift, or fissure, started to open; in essence, the tectonic plates were literally splitting Rodinia apart. This geological event is known as the Midcontinent Rift.

Molten rock began to rise and fill the widening gap. But the rift failed and the spreading stopped, leaving almost 500,000 cubic miles of volcanic rock that spans several states. If the rift had succeeded, Minnesota would likely border an ocean today. In Minnesota, these ancient rocks extend from the Canadian border in northeastern Minnesota, through the Twin Cities area, and across the Iowa border, though they are only easily visible on the beaches of Minnesota's North Shore of Lake Superior as dense gray pebbles, cliffs and ledges of rock

A lot of interesting minerals formed within the volcanic Midcontinent Rift rocks, particularly inside the vesicles (gas bubbles) trapped in basalt (page 87) and rhyolite (page 193), the two most common rocks that formed in the event. It is in this setting that the famous Lake Superior agates (page 35) formed, as well as the delicate crystals of quartz (page 185), calcite (page 91), epidote (page 117), feldspars (page 119) and thomsonite-(Ca) (page 211) that are found in Minnesota's basalt. And luckily for rock hounds, the glaciers and Lake Superior's waves have done the hard work of breaking many of these collectibles out of the rock, which makes northeastern Minnesota the perfect place for novice rock collectors to start their new hobby. If you're planning to hunt for rocks and minerals in this region, Lake Superior's shore is the best and easiest place to start, as are the banks of rivers connecting with the lake. Also, any gravel in the region was deposited by the glaciers that scoured the rocks; this glacial till can yield agates and other collectibles, which are buried in dirt piles and on beaches of small inland lakes.

Inland Seas and the Twin Cities

Minnesota may not seem a likely place to find specimens of fossil coral or shark teeth, but those are just two reminders of Minnesota's aquatic past. The enormous formations of sandstone (page 195), limestone (page 157) and shale (page 197) that underlie Minneapolis and St. Paul are another impressive legacy of Minnesota's ancient seas. These types of rocks are sedimentary and formed in large bodies of water; over the past billion years there have been plenty of opportunities for them to form and survive in the Twin Cities area.

Further geological activity following the Midcontinent Rift caused the newly formed volcanic rocks to sag and form a depression in which water and sediment could collect, forming lakes. As a result, all of the Midcontinent Rift rocks, including those under the Twin Cities, were buried under sedimentary rocks. In addition, as the earth changed and the continents moved, there were many periods when Minnesota was inundated by shallow inland seas. The first of these existed approximately 475 million years ago while the most recent may have been present as recently as 65 million years ago. Each of these seas also deposited thick beds of sediment that later formed rocks. By the time the last sea subsided, several thousand feet of sedimentary rocks covered Minnesota. Then, as recently as 10,000 years ago, glaciers pulverized the soft sedimentary rocks situated along modern-day Lake Superior's shore and once again exposed the hard Midcontinent Rift rocks in northeastern Minnesota. But in the southern half of the state, including the Twin Cities area, thick layers of sedimentary rocks remain.

Today, the Mississippi River cuts through the sedimentary rocks and provides some interesting views of the soft, layered sandstones and shales right in the center of the Twin Cities area. And while most people wouldn't think that such a heavily populated area could be a rock hunter's destination, you may be surprised at how many minerals can be found there. Thanks in part to both the Mississippi River and the glaciers, many of the interesting minerals from northern Minnesota, including agates, have been transported south and can be found in the Twin Cities area, both in rivers and gravel pits. In addition, formations of shale are present along the Mississippi River, especially near downtown St. Paul, and fossils (page 123) and various other minerals, such as pyrite (page 179), can be found when the shale's soft layers are carefully separated.

Rocks and Minerals Found in the Twin Cities

Some rock hounds assume that Minnesota's collectible rocks and minerals are found only in specific and far-flung locations, such as Lake Superior's North Shore, or in one of the state's iron ranges. While this is sometimes true, many interesting rocks and minerals can be found in the Twin Cities area. To call attention to these potential finds, we've labeled them on each rock or mineral's respective page. To determine whether or not a mineral is found in the Twin Cities area, look for this outline of a skyline in the bottom right-hand corner of a given account about a rock or mineral.

Glaciers and Glacial Lakes

One of the most recent, yet most important, events that shaped Minnesota's landscape was the appearance of glaciers during the ice ages. As is clear by the lack of sedimentary rocks in northeastern Minnesota, the incredible weight of the glaciers crushed and scraped away untold amounts of rock as the glaciers descended from Canada. Periods of warm weather caused the glaciers to melt and temporarily retreat north, only to move south again when temperatures dropped. This repeated movement acted like a bulldozer, gradually shaving away rock and dumping it all over the state as gravel called glacial till. As a result, areas of northern Minnesota exhibit exposed bedrock, such as the Midcontinent Rift rocks on the

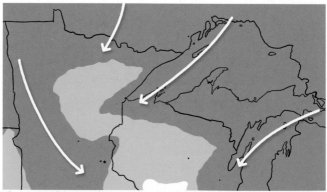

The extent of the last glaciers is shown in brown and their direction of movement is shown by the arrows. The extent of older glaciers is in tan.

North Shore, as well as huge glacial till formations where weathered mineral specimens, like agates, can be found. Inland lakes and rivers also expose loosely compacted glacial till, where digging to find specimens of chalcedony (page 95), jasper (page 151) and copper (page 111) is easy.

As the glaciers retreated for the last time, thousands of giant, isolated blocks of ice broke off and melted, each creating one of Minnesota's many lakes. But all paled in comparison to Glacial Lake Agassiz, one of the largest lakes ever to exist. Lake Agassiz covered a huge area in Canada and northern Minnesota, but was relatively short-lived and turned into smaller lakes as it drained to the Hudson Bay. Today, Lake of the Woods, the Red River Valley and the Minnesota River are remnants of Lake Agassiz. With the movement of so much water over sedimentary rock, riverbanks and farm fields in western and southwestern Minnesota yield specimens of gypsum (page 143), barite (page 85) and calcite (page 91), all of which are easy to acquire when one diligently and carefully digs through mud and clay.

Iron Ranges and Mining Districts

The rocks formed during the Midcontinent Rift are ancient, but other formations are even older. Between 2.5 and 1.6 billion years ago, Minnesota experienced a period of geological stability; this allowed large amounts of iron-rich sediments to settle into the Animikie Basin, an enormous body of water stretching northeast from central Minnesota into Canada. Along with sediments rich in silica (quartz material), these iron particles began to form thin layers. As the eons passed and the layers were gradually buried and compressed, long but relatively narrow formations of rocks rich in iron minerals formed. Called iron ranges, these bodies of prehistoric rock contain large amounts of hematite (page 145), goethite (page 131) and other iron ores (minerals from which iron is obtained).

There are three iron ranges in Minnesota that formed from sediments at the bottom of the Animikie Basin. The Mesabi Iron Range in northeastern Minnesota is the biggest range in the state and is the only one that still supports an active mining industry. The Cuyuna range is closer to central Minnesota and the Vermilion Iron Range is near the Canadian border in northeastern Minnesota; it owes part of its formation to volcanic activity. Eager rock hounds can visit all three in hopes of finding specimens of iron minerals, but most of the Mesabi Range is off-limits due to privately owned and actively mined land. In the other two iron ranges, mine dumps, also called tailing piles, can be found; this is where the old mining operations dumped their unwanted waste rock. In many piles, hematite, goethite and magnetite (page 163) are easily found. The Cuyuna Iron Range's mine dumps also contain unique manganese ores, such as rhodochrosite (page 191), one of the most uniquely colored minerals in the state.

Summary

While this brief summary only scratches the surface of Minnesota's incredible geological past, you now have some

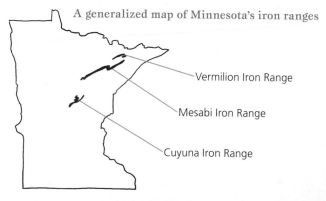

A generalized map of Minnesota's iron ranges

Vermilion Iron Range

Mesabi Iron Range

Cuyuna Iron Range

knowledge of the most significant rock and mineral collecting regions of Minnesota and how they came to be. This will help in determining where certain minerals can be found.

Precautions

It may be surprising, but there are some risks inherent in rock and mineral collecting. Please be aware that it is always your responsibility to know where you legally can (or cannot) collect, which minerals may be hazardous to your health, and what you need to take with you in order to be prepared for any difficulties you may face.

Protected and Private Land

Minnesota has dozens of state parks and forests, Native American reservations and nationally protected parks and monuments, all of which are areas where it is illegal to collect anything. Large fines await those caught collecting in protected areas. We encourage collectors to obey the law and leave these natural spaces wild and untouched for generations to come. It is your responsibility to know whether or not the area in which you are collecting is protected. In addition, many potential collecting sites are privately owned, including many parts of Minnesota's Lake Superior shoreline. Needless to say, if you collect on private property you are trespassing, and the penalty may be worse than just a fine. In addition, property lines change frequently, as do owners, so just because a landowner gave you permission to collect on their property last year it doesn't mean that the new owner will allow you on their property the next year. Finally, Minnesota's iron mining industry is still very active, and though it may be tempting to venture onto mining land and look through their material, this is not only foolish, but completely illegal. Mining operations and railroads are private property, and even walking along a railroad track can result in a citation for trespassing.

Collecting Etiquette

When you wish to collect on privately owned land, you should always attempt to contact the landowner. If you have obtained permission to dig on someone's property, you should respect their generosity and leave the site in the condition you found it. Too often sites are closed to collectors because of vandalism, littering and indiscriminate digging. If a site is on public land where collecting is allowed, the same rules apply, otherwise the state may close the area. Being a courteous and respectful collector will ensure great, accessible collecting sites for everyone.

Dangerous Places

While collecting rocks and minerals in Minnesota, there is a good chance you'll come across some dangerous territory. The shore of Lake Superior, popular among collectors, is lined with tall cliffs and sea caverns, often with highly weathered and crumbly rock. In addition, the southeastern corner of Minnesota is known for its "karst topography," a landscape that consists of soft rock that is prone to producing sinkholes and caves. While the odds of a sinkhole opening beneath your feet are slim, you should never enter a cave produced by these events as they can be highly unstable and are liable to collapse, especially in rainy weather. In addition, many mining areas in Minnesota are still active, and the equipment, explosives and risk of arrest make it obvious that you should stay away. But other mining regions do contain mine dumps, or large piles of waste rock left over from mining that are often unattended and overgrown. These piles can be great for collecting, but can also be unstable and dangerous. When climbing a mine dump, be careful not to start a slide of jagged rock crashing onto everything below. Similarly, gravel pits are also favored by collectors, but they are often privately owned and contain highly unstable piles and cliffs of gravel which can—and will—collapse as a result of strong wind, rain or a careless rock hound. This is especially true in gravel pits that are worked on a regular basis.

Equipment and Supplies

When you set out to collect rocks and minerals, there are a few items you don't want to forget. No matter where you are collecting, leather gloves are a good idea, as are knee pads if you plan to spend a lot of time on the ground. If you think you'll be breaking rock, bring your rock hammer (not a nail hammer) and eye protection. If the weather is hot and sunny, take the proper precautions and use sunblock and bring sunglasses and a hat, as well as ample water, both for drinking and for rinsing specimens. Lastly, a global positioning system (GPS) device is a great way to prevent you from getting lost.

 Potentially Hazardous Minerals

Many states have dozens of minerals that can be hazardous to human health, but luckily Minnesota has very few. Marked by the symbol shown above, the amphibole group (page 75) contains several minerals that can occur in the form of asbestos, a type of mineral crystallization with tiny hair-like fibers, which are fabric-like, flexible and can easily become airborne. If inhaled, these minerals pose a cancer risk. If you come across any mineral that appears to have loose fibers, wear a dust mask or respirator to lessen the risk of inhalation, or avoid it altogether.

Hardness and Streak

There are two important techniques everyone wishing to identify minerals should know: hardness and streak tests. All minerals will yield results in both tests, as will certain rocks, which makes these tests indispensable to collectors.

The measure of how resistant a mineral is to abrasion is called hardness. The most common hardness scale, called the Mohs hardness scale, ranges from 1 to 10, with 10 being the hardest. An example of a mineral with a hardness of 1 is talc; it is a chalky mineral that can easily be scratched by your fingernail. An example of a mineral with a hardness of 10 is diamond, which is the hardest naturally occurring substance on earth and will scratch every other mineral. Most minerals, including most of Minnesota's, fall somewhere in the range of 2 to 7 on the Mohs hardness scale, so learning how to perform a hardness test (also known as a scratch test) is critical. Common tools used in a hardness test include your fingernail, a U.S. nickel, a piece of glass and a steel pocket knife. There are also hardness kits you can purchase that have a tool of each hardness.

To perform a scratch test, you simply scratch a mineral with a tool of a known hardness—for example, we know a steel knife has a hardness of about 5.5. If the mineral is not scratched, you will then move to a tool of greater hardness until the mineral is scratched. If a tool that is 6.5 in hardness scratches your specimen, but a 5.5 does not, you can conclude that your mineral is a 6 in hardness. Two tips to consider: As you will be putting a scratch on the specimen, perform the test on the backside of the piece (or, better yet, on a lower-quality specimen of the same mineral), and start with tools softer in hardness and work your way up. On page 18, you'll find a chart that shows which tools will scratch a mineral of a particular hardness.

The second test every amateur geologist and rock collector should know is streak. When a mineral is crushed or powdered, it will have a distinct color—this color is the same as the streak color. When a mineral is rubbed along a streak plate, it will leave behind a powdery stripe of color, called the streak. This is an important test to perform because sometimes the streak color will differ greatly from the mineral itself. Hematite, for example, is a dark, metallic and gray mineral, yet its streak is a rusty red color. Streak plates are sold in some rock and mineral shops, but if you cannot find one, a simple unglazed piece of porcelain from a hardware store will work. There are only two things you need to remember about streak tests: If the mineral is harder than the streak plate, it will not produce a streak and will instead scratch the plate itself. Secondly, don't bother testing rocks for streak; they are made up of many different minerals and won't produce a consistent color.

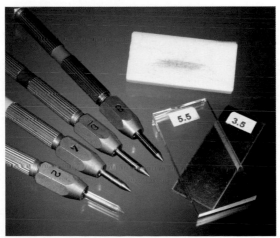

Tools from a professional hardness kit

The Mohs Hardness Scale

The Mohs hardness scale is the primary measure of mineral hardness. This scale ranges from 1 to 10, from softest to hardest. Ten minerals commonly associated with the scale are listed here, as well as some common tools used to determine a mineral's hardness. If a mineral is scratched by a tool of a known hardness, then you know it is softer than that tool.

HARDNESS	EXAMPLE MINERAL	TOOL
1	Talc	
2	Gypsum	
2.5		Fingernail
3	Calcite	
3.5		U.S. nickel/brass
4	Fluorite	
5	Apatite	
5.5		Glass, steel knife
6	Orthoclase feldspar	
6.5		Streak plate
7	Quartz	
7.5		Hardened steel file
8	Topaz	
9	Corundum	
9.5		Silicon carbide
10	Diamond	

For example, if a mineral is scratched by a U.S. nickel but not your fingernail, you can conclude that its hardness is 3, equal to that of calcite. If a mineral is harder than 6.5, or the hardness of a streak plate, it will have no streak and will instead scratch the streak plate itself, unless weathered to a softer state.

Quick Identification Guide

Use this quick identification guide to help you determine which rock or mineral you may have found. We've listed the primary color groups and some basic characteristics of the rocks and minerals of Minnesota, as well as the page number where you can read more about your possible find. While the most common traits for each rock or mineral are listed here, be aware that your specimen may differ greatly.

	If white or colorless and...	then try...
	Ball-like crystals within cavities in basalt, often with an orange or red stain	analcime, page 77
	Six-sided elongated crystals, often with a flat tip, which can't be scratched with a U.S. nickel	aragonite, page 81
	Soft, abundant six-sided crystals or blocky masses within other rock, particularly basalt	calcite, page 91
	Hard masses with a cauliflower-like outer texture and porcelain-like interiors	datolite, page 113
	Glassy, blocky masses found abundantly within rocks	feldspar group, page 119
	Extremely soft, glassy rectangular crystals easily scratched by your fingernail	gypsum, page 143
	Very abundant six-sided crystals or masses that are very hard	quartz, page 185

WHITE OR COLORLESS

Quick Identification Guide (continued)

(continued) **If white or colorless and...**	**then try...**
Very hard, solid rock with a grainy appearance and slight translucence	quartzite, page 189

GRAY

If gray and...	**then try...**
Very coarse rock with many glassy, translucent masses	anorthosite, page 79
Extremely common, dark-colored rock often found on the lakeshore	basalt, page 87
Very hard, opaque masses of rock that are waxy in appearance if weathered	chert, page 99
Dense, gray rock with a mottled appearance exhibiting lighter spots	diabase, page 115
Light-colored rock abundant along Lake Superior, often with many vesicles (gas bubbles)	rhyolite, page 193
Extremely hard, dense, opaque rock that is magnetic	taconite, page 209

Quick Identification Guide (continued)

BLACK

	If black and...	then try...
	Hard grains or masses with a silky sheen that are embedded within rocks	amphibole group, page 75
	Dark, very coarse rock containing grains of many black minerals	gabbro, page 125
	Compact, dark rock often with thin layers and shiny flecks of mica	schist, page 129
	Metallic, heavy mineral with rounded surfaces or fibrous structure and a brownish yellow streak	goethite, page 131
	Rounded crusts of a hard, metallic mineral with a reddish streak	hematite, page 145
	Hard grains that stick strongly to a magnet	magnetite, page 163
	Glassy, blocky crystals within dark-colored rocks, especially gabbro	pyroxene group, page 183
	Hard, brittle rock found in tightly compacted layers that can be separated	slate, page 197
	Very hard, slender, striated (grooved) crystals, often embedded in rock	tourmaline group, page 213

Quick Identification Guide (continued)

	If blue and...	then try...
	Soft, crumbly masses, usually alongside copper or green malachite	chrysocolla, page 103

YELLOW

	If yellow and...	then try...
	Very hard, waxy pebbles found on the lakeshore	chert, page 99
	Tiny, rare, ball-like crystals in cavities alongside green minerals	garnet group, page 127
	Dull, earthy masses of rust-colored material that often leave a yellow dust on your hands after handling	limonite, page 159

GREEN

	If green and...	then try...
	Elongated, fibrous crystals embedded in rock	amphibole group, page 75
	Very common, soft, dark mineral typically found lining cavities in rocks	chlorite, page 101
	Yellowish green, very glassy and reflective tiny crystals, often in cavities within basalt	epidote, page 117

(continued)	**If green and...**	then try...
	Soft, glassy mineral with angular surfaces and cracks	fluorite, page 121
	Green layers within large masses of very hard, banded rock	greenalite, page 137
	Dense, compact rock only found in northern Minnesota	greenstone, page 139
	Round, gray-green pebbles found on Lake Superior's shore	lintonite, page 161
	Soft, vividly colored masses, typically alongside copper or blue chrysocolla	malachite, page 165
	Soft, bluish coatings or masses within vesicles (gas bubbles) in basalt	mica group, page 171
	Hard, glassy, translucent grains or masses within rock, particularly gabbro	olivine group, page 175
	Very hard, botryoidal (grape-like) masses with a fibrous cross section typically found in basalt	prehnite, page 177

GREEN

Quick Identification Guide (continued)

BROWN

	If brown and...	then try...
	Rough, very hard, rounded masses with dimpled surfaces	agate, page 35
	Waxy, rounded masses of translucent material, often with black spots	southern Minnesota agate, page 63
	Rough, rocky spheres containing pockets of colorful banding inside when broken	thunder egg, page 65
	Translucent, glassy blade-like crystals that feel heavy for their size	barite, page 85
	Abundant, soft, gritty material that is crumbly when dry but malleable and sticky when wet	clay, page 105
	Compact spheres of rock, often found embedded in soft rock	concretions, page 107
	Rocks containing what appears to be teeth, shells or coral	fossils, page 123
	Hard, metallic mineral often with rust-like coatings and a fibrous cross section	goethite, page 131
	Abundant, soft rock that fizzes in vinegar	limestone, page 157

Quick Identification Guide (continued)

(continued) **If brown and...**	**then try...**
Flexible, translucent flakes arranged into parallel layers	mica group, page 171
Gritty, extremely fine-grained rock, often with chert	mudstone or siltstone, page 173
Grainy, very rough rock consisting of grains of sand easily separated with your hands	sandstone, page 195
Fine-grained rock consisting of thin, compact layers easily separated in sheets	shale, page 197
Soft crystals or masses with an angular, blocky appearance and often occurring alongside goethite	siderite, page 199
Very hard, rectangular crystals with a diamond-shaped cross section	staurolite, page 203
Very hard, solid rock with a grainy appearance and slight translucence	quartzite, page 189

BROWN

If red and...	**then try...**
Soft, compact rock only found in southwestern Minnesota	catlinite, page 93

RED

Quick Identification Guide (continued)

	(continued) **If red and...**	**then try...**
	Very hard, rounded crystals, often found at river bottoms	garnet group, page 127
	Hard, metallic masses, often with a botryoidal (grape-like) structure	hematite, page 145
	Very hard, opaque material, often found as waxy, smooth masses on lakeshore	jasper, page 151
	Very soft, dusty material that easily turns your fingers red after handling	red ochre, page 159
	Very hard, abundant, six-sided crystals often found in mine dumps	quartz, page 187
	Reddish abundant rock found along Lake Superior's shore, often with darker stripes	rhyolite, page 193

RED

	If orange and...	**then try...**
	Hard, blocky crystals growing within cracks or cavities in rock	feldspar group, page 119
	Very soft, crumbly, rectangular crystals in basalt and often with calcite	laumontite, page 155

ORANGE

Quick Identification Guide (continued)

(continued) **If orange and...**	**then try...**
Rare, soft crystal groupings resembling a sheaf of wheat or a bow-tie	stilbite, page 205

ORANGE

If violet or pink and...	**then try...**
Soft, glassy mineral with angular surfaces and cracks	fluorite, page 121
Very hard, six-sided crystals or masses	quartz varieties, page 187
Soft, blocky masses or crystals found in mine dumps in central Minnesota	rhodochrosite, page 191
Pebbles or masses with radial or circular arrangements of needle-like crystals	thomsonite-(Ca), page 211

VIOLET OR PINK

If metallic and...	**then try...**
Bright yellow mineral, often with a colorful surface coating, embedded in rocks, particularly gabbro	chalcopyrite, page 97
Soft, very flexible sheets or nuggets of reddish metal	copper, page 111

METALLIC

Quick Identification Guide (continued)

(continued)	**If metallic and...**	**then try...**
	Very soft and flexible yellow flecks embedded within quartz or as grains in rivers	gold, page 133
	Brightly reflective, black, curving blade-like crystals found in mine dumps in central Minnesota	groutite, page 141
	Black grains or masses that are slightly magnetic and found in sand or embedded in rock	ilmenite, page 149
	Very lightweight silvery "blobs" of metal on the lakeshore	junk, page 153
	Shiny black masses that are strongly magnetic	magnetite, page 163
	Blocky or bladed crystals found in mine dumps in central Minnesota	manganite, page 167
	Hard, brass-colored masses or crystal groups resembling serrations with striated (grooved) surfaces	marcasite, page 169
	Cubes or masses of a hard, brassy mineral, often embedded in rocks	pyrite, page 179
	Shiny black veins or masses consisting of a very fibrous mineral that leaves your hands black after handling	pyrolusite, page 181

METALLIC

METALLIC

(continued) **If metallic and...**	**then try...**
Silvery or gray veins tightly embedded in quartz	silver, page 201

MULTICOLORED OR BANDED

If multicolored or banded and...	**then try...**
Very hard masses consisting of concentric rings of color	agate, page 35
Lumpy, rounded masses with a banded or layered cross section	coldwater agate, page 39
Very hard masses containing circular, ring-like sections	eye agate, page 41
Very hard masses containing both quartz crystals and concentric rings of color	floater agate, page 45
Very hard masses exhibiting concentric rings of color as well as broken, curving, soft fragments	fragmented membrane agate, page 47
Very hard masses consisting of concentric rings of color surrounding a hollow center	agate geode, page 49
Very hard masses containing parallel, horizontal layering	gravitationally banded agate, page 51

(continued)	**If multicolored or banded and...**	**then try...**
	Very hard masses containing irregular, plant-like growths of color	moss agate, page 53
	Very hard masses containing concentric banding in opaque shades of pink, orange and tan	paint agate, page 55
	Very hard masses containing concentric banding and radial "sprays" of needle-like crystals	sagenitic agate, page 59
	Very hard masses containing colored bands as well as fragmented, opaque bluish gray crystals	skip-an-atom agate, page 61
	Rough, brown, spherical rocks containing orange and red banded patterns within	thunder egg, page 65
	Very hard masses containing concentric banding as well as long structures resembling tunnels or tubes	tube agate, page 67
	Very hard elongated masses, often embedded in rock, which contain concentric banding	vein agate, page 69
	Very hard masses containing wavy, overlapping bands of color	whorl agate, page 73
	Very hard, dense rock containing parallel layers that can be any combination of red, black, white, yellow or green	banded iron formation, page 83

MULTICOLORED OR BANDED

Quick Identification Guide (continued)

MULTICOLORED OR BANDED

(continued)	**If multicolored or banded and...**	**then try...**
	Hard masses of white, red and black material with fibrous yellow sections	binghamite or silkstone, page 89
	Very hard translucent masses of mottled, uneven coloration	chalcedony, page 95
	Rocks clearly consisting of other rocks or rock fragments embedded in a fine-grained material	conglomerate or breccia, page 109
	Hard, dense rock with a coarsely banded appearance	gneiss, page 129
	Very coarse rock with mottled coloration, often predominantly light colored with small dark spots	granite, page 135
	Shiny, botryoidal (grape-like) surfaces with a rainbow-like iridescence	hematite varieties, page 147
	Very hard, opaque masses with layers of color in shades of red, yellow and green	jasper, page 151
	Very hard rocks with rounded, wavy, sometimes mushroom-shaped layered structures	stromatolite, page 207

Rough specimens

"Moss" growths

Close-up of moss

Polished specimen

Small section
of agate
bands

Sample Page

HARDNESS: 7 **STREAK:** White

Occurrence

ENVIRONMENT: A generalized indication of the
types of places where this rock or mineral
can commonly be found by collectors; for
the purposes of this book, the primary environments
listed include lakeshore, riverbeds (and riverbanks), gravel
pits, road cuts (where roads have been cut through hills),
mine dumps (large piles of waste rock left over at the
sites of many mines), and fields (which includes low-lying
grasslands, farm fields, or other flat regions)

WHAT TO LOOK FOR: Common and characteristic identifying traits
of the rock or mineral

SIZE: The general size range of the rock or mineral; the listed
sizes apply more to minerals and their crystals than to rocks,
which typically form in large masses

COLOR: The general colors the rock or mineral exhibits in its
natural state

OCCURRENCE: The difficulty of finding this rock or mineral;
"very common" means the material takes almost no effort
to find; "common" means the material can be found with
little effort; "uncommon" means the material may take
a good deal of hunting to find; "rare" means finding the
material will take a good deal of research, time and energy;
"very rare" means the material is so uncommon that you
will be lucky to find even a trace of it

NOTES: Additional information about the rock or mineral, includ
ing how to find it, how to identify it, how to distinguish it
from similar minerals and interesting facts about it.

WHERE TO LOOK: Specific regions or towns that are good places
to begin your search for the rock or mineral.

Beach-worn agates

Common agate "chips"

Waxy luster

Conchoidal fracture

Agate in basalt

Whole, unbroken agates

Agate formed in two connected vesicles

Green surface coating

Agate

HARDNESS: 7 **STREAK:** White

Occurrence

ENVIRONMENT: Lakeshore, riverbeds, fields, gravel pits, road cuts

WHAT TO LOOK FOR: Very hard, translucent, red or brown rounded masses of material containing ring-like bands within

SIZE: Agates range from pea-sized fragments to fist-sized nodules

COLOR: Multicolored; varies greatly, but banding is primarily red, brown, orange, white or gray

OCCURRENCE: Uncommon

NOTES: Lake Superior agates, the beautifully banded stones from Lake Superior's shore, are undoubtedly Minnesota's most popular and best-known collectible mineral. But agates are also one of the world's most mysterious mineral growths. Despite over 300 years of research, we have only a basic understanding of how they form, and many details of their genesis are still unknown. But while we don't know exactly what causes their characteristic concentric banding, we do know that agates are composed of layered chalcedony (a variety of quartz), and formed in vesicles (gas bubbles) in volcanic rocks, particularly basalt. As a form of quartz (page 185), agates have similar characteristics, including high hardness, translucency and conchoidal fracture (when struck, circular cracks appear). In addition, agates have a waxy appearance and texture when broken. But it is important to remember that agates form layer by layer and only show banding when broken, whole agates simply look like hard, rounded stones, often with a rough, pitted surface.

WHERE TO LOOK: The shores of Lake Superior and northern inland lakes are popular, but many agates also come out of riverbeds in northeastern Minnesota and private gravel pits near Cloquet. Farm fields all over the state are great, too.

Polished specimens

Rough specimen

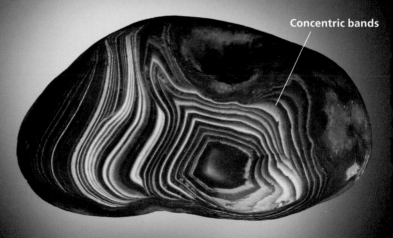

Concentric bands

Rough specimen

Agate, Adhesional Banded

HARDNESS: 7 **STREAK:** White

Occurrence

ENVIRONMENT: Lakeshore, riverbeds, fields, gravel pits, road cuts

WHAT TO LOOK FOR: Very hard, reddish brown rounded masses of material containing band-within-a-band patterning

SIZE: Agates range from pea-sized fragments to fist-sized nodules

COLOR: Multicolored; varies greatly, but banding is primarily red, brown, orange, white or gray

OCCURRENCE: Uncommon

NOTES: There are many types of Lake Superior agates, but adhesional banded agates are the most common, famous and valuable variety. Known among collectors as fortification agates because their banded patterns often resemble the concentric walls of a fort or castle, adhesional banded agates exhibit quintessential agate banding—a repeating pattern in which interior bands appear to adhere to outer bands. LIke the skin of an onion, each layer of banding surrounds interior layers until the center of the agate is reached. This uninterrupted layering process (and the concentric banding pattern that comes with it) is the hallmark of an adhesional banded agate. Occasionally, due to a drop in the amount of silica (quartz compound) available to an agate during its formation, the center of a specimen may consist of large quartz crystals instead of banding. Finally, the coloration in all agates is caused by various impurities—reds and browns are caused by hematite, yellows by goethite and gray by microscopic water bubbles.

WHERE TO LOOK: Some of the finest specimens have come from farm fields, riverbeds and lakeshore near Two Harbors, Knife River and Beaver Bay, as well as from privately owned gravel pits near Cloquet and other areas near Duluth.

Coldwater agate

Quartz crystal coating

Specimen courtesy of Phil Burgess

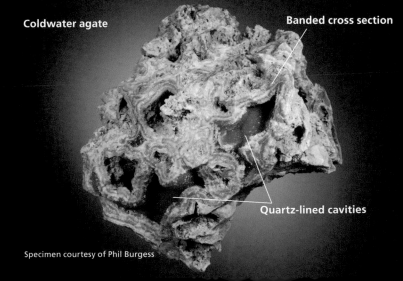

Coldwater agate

Banded cross section

Quartz-lined cavities

Specimen courtesy of Phil Burgess

Agate, Coldwater

HARDNESS: 7 **STREAK:** White

Occurrence

ENVIRONMENT: Riverbeds, fields, gravel pits, road cuts

WHAT TO LOOK FOR: Very hard, rough, irregular masses consisting of hollow, crystal-lined pockets surrounded by banding

SIZE: Coldwater agates range in size from thumbnail-sized specimens to those that are basketball-sized and rarely larger

COLOR: Multicolored; varies greatly, but banding is primarily white, gray, bluish gray or brown

OCCURRENCE: Rare

NOTES: Minnesota is best known for Lake Superior agates, but they are not Minnesota's only agates. Coldwater agates, which are found in southeastern Minnesota, are named for their unique formation. Coldwater agates formed when water bearing silica (quartz compound) seeped down and accumulated within cavities and pores in various materials, particularly limestone, a soft sedimentary rock. This water originated on the earth's surface and likely came from ancient seas; it was therefore cold, giving coldwater agates their name. By comparison, Lake Superior agates formed when solutions of warm volcanic water rose from the earth and filled vesicles (gas bubbles) within basalt and rhyolite. Often coldwater agates replaced the material in which they formed. For example, the specimens shown here were once composed of limestone that contained fossils of stromatolites (page 207), but as the silica accumulated and the limestone dissolved, only the hard, rough agate remains.

WHERE TO LOOK: There aren't many locations, but gravel pits and riverbeds in Winona and Houston Counties, along the Mississippi River in the southeast corner of the state, have yielded specimens.

Rough specimens

Detail of eye

Inset specimen courtesy of
Christopher Cordes

Polished specimens

Agate, Eye

HARDNESS: 7 **STREAK:** White

ENVIRONMENT: Lakeshore, riverbeds, fields, gravel pits, road cuts

Occurrence

WHAT TO LOOK FOR: Very hard, reddish brown rounded masses of material containing perfectly circular banded structures

SIZE: Eye agates are typically smaller than your palm

COLOR: Multicolored; varies greatly, but banding is primarily red, brown, orange, white and gray

OCCURRENCE: Uncommon

NOTES: Often called "fish eyes," eye agates are a unique variety of Lake Superior agate. They contain small, perfectly circular banded spots that resemble eyes. The eyes are actually hemispheres, or half-spheres, that formed on the outer surface and extend inward like a shallow bowl. While it's not exactly clear how eye agates form and existing theories are quite complicated, we do know that eyes typically only occur on smaller agates, generally on specimens no larger than your palm and often as small as a pea. It is hypothesized that agates that formed in small vesicles (gas bubbles) may have had access to more silica (quartz compound) than they needed. (Larger agates obviously need more silica.) It is thought that the excess silica continued to interact with the agate even after it had finished forming, enlarging certain tiny features until they grew into large, visible eyes. Eye agates, though generally easy to identify, can be easily confused with tube agates (page 67), but tubes are long, cylindrical structures that extend through an agate.

WHERE TO LOOK: The shores of Lake Superior and northern inland lakes are the most popular hunting grounds for eye agates, but they are also found in gravel pits near Cloquet.

Polished "ruin" agate

Faulted banding

Large agate fragments

Quartz

Rough brecciated agate

Agate, Faulted

HARDNESS: 7 **STREAK:** White

Occurrence

ENVIRONMENT: Lakeshore, riverbeds, fields, gravel pits, road cuts

WHAT TO LOOK FOR: Very hard, reddish rounded masses of material containing bands that appear broken or interrupted

SIZE: Specimens range from pea-sized fragments to fist-sized nodules

COLOR: Multicolored; varies greatly, but banding primarily occurs in red, brown, orange, white or gray

OCCURRENCE: Uncommon

NOTES: At 1.1 billion years old, Lake Superior's agates are among the oldest agates on earth. But nothing survives such inconceivable lengths of time unscathed. Most agates show some kind of damage or weathering as a result of the immense glaciers that crushed and transported them, but faulted agates were actually damaged before they were freed from their host rock. Earthquakes and volcanic activity were likely responsible for cracking, crushing and shifting these agates. After the destructive event, solutions containing silica (quartz compound) "healed" the broken agate, resulting in agates with faults, or sections of banding that don't quite match or fit together. Some agates were less lucky, however, and were crushed entirely before they were re-formed into a solid mass. These are called brecciated agates, and contain fragments of completely disjointed banding. Collectors favor "ruin" agates, which tend to have faulted agate banding on their edges and agate breccia at the center.

WHERE TO LOOK: There is no telling where a faulted or brecciated agate may turn up. The usual hunting grounds—riverbeds and lakeshore on Lake Superior and gravel pits near Duluth and Cloquet—are good places to look.

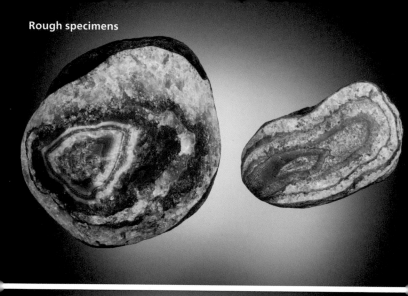

Rough specimens

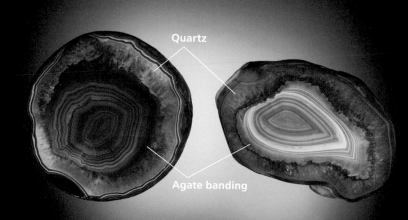

Quartz

Agate banding

Polished specimens

Agate, Floater

HARDNESS: 7 **STREAK:** White

Occurrence

ENVIRONMENT: Lakeshore, riverbeds, fields, gravel pits, road cuts

WHAT TO LOOK FOR: Very hard, reddish rounded masses of material containing agate banding surrounded by quartz crystals

SIZE: Agates range from pea-sized fragments to fist-sized nodules

COLOR: Multicolored; varies greatly, but banding is primarily red, brown, orange, white or gray

OCCURRENCE: Uncommon

NOTES: When agates form within a vesicle (gas bubble), they need a steadily replenished supply of silica, the quartz compound from which agates are formed. Adhesional banded agates develop when the supply of silica to the vesicle is steady and uninterrupted, but floater agates result when the silica supply is not constant. While the full details of this process can be very complicated, it is important to note that chalcedony, the variety of quartz of which agate bands are composed, requires much more silica (quartz compound) to form than coarse quartz crystals do (page 185). So when an agate contains a central region of agate banding surrounded by quartz crystals, that means that there were dramatic changes in the amount of silica available during the agate's formation. Popular among collectors, floater agates get their name because an island of banded chalcedony appears to be "floating" in a "sea" of quartz. Floaters with alternating bands of chalcedony and quartz are also common, creating several "floating" portions of an agate.

WHERE TO LOOK: As with any variety of Lake Superior agate, the shores of Lake Superior and inland lakes are popular, as well as riverbeds in northeastern Minnesota and private gravel pits near Cloquet.

Polished specimen

Rough specimen

Agate banding

Polished specimen

Membrane fragments

Agate, Fragmented Membrane

Occurrence

HARDNESS: 7 **STREAK:** White

ENVIRONMENT: Lakeshore, riverbeds, fields, gravel pits, road cuts

WHAT TO LOOK FOR: Very hard, reddish brown rounded masses of material containing curving, ribbon-like fragments

SIZE: Agates range from pea-sized fragments to fist-sized nodules

COLOR: Multicolored; varies greatly, but banding is primarily red, brown, orange, white or gray

OCCURRENCE: Uncommon

NOTES: Basalt, the rock in which Lake Superior agates primarily develop, forms when lava, or molten rock, spills onto the earth's surface and cools rapidly. Lava contains enormous amounts of gases that are then trapped as vesicles, or gas bubbles, in the cooling, solidifying rock. The gases trapped inside the solid, but still warm, rock then begin to react with the minerals in the rock itself, creating new minerals in the process. A thin lining or membrane of minerals such as chlorite (page 101) or celadonite (page 171) results and forms on the inner walls of the vesicle. An agate can then form within such a membrane, but sometimes the mineral lining is broken and fragmented, causing it to peel away from the walls and fall into the developing agate. Entombed within chalcedony, the thin, curving, ribbon-like fragments often occur only in one half of an agate and make for unique, instantly recognizable specimens appropriately called "fragmented membrane agates." As the fragments consist of minerals much softer than quartz, they often weather more easily than the agate, causing them to appear pitted and recessed.

WHERE TO LOOK: As with any Lake Superior agates, there are no definite locations, though gravel pits near Cloquet are good.

Rough specimen

Quartz-lined cavities

Polished specimen

Rough specimens

Quartz-lined center

Calcite mass

Agate, Geode

HARDNESS: 7 **STREAK:** White

ENVIRONMENT: Lakeshore, riverbeds, fields, gravel pits, road cuts

Occurrence

WHAT TO LOOK FOR: Very hard, reddish rounded masses of material containing ring-like bands and a hollow center

SIZE: Agates range from pea-sized fragments to fist-sized nodules

COLOR: Multicolored; varies greatly, but banding is primarily red, brown, orange, white and gray

OCCURRENCE: Rare

NOTES: A geode is a round and hollow mass of material, and geodes are well known among collectors for sometimes containing beautiful crystals growing in the space inside. However, this definition is rather loose and encompasses many different kinds of hollow rock and mineral formations. Most geodes around the world are composed of soft rocks, like limestone, but in the Lake Superior region, agate geodes can be found. Lake Superior agate geodes are certainly a curious find for Minnesota rock hounds, but their formation is easily understood. When agates are forming within a vesicle (gas bubble), they need a steady supply of silica (quartz compound), the material from which agates and quartz are formed. If the supply of silica is interrupted, agate formation ceases, and if the supply is never replenished, the agate remains "incomplete" and hollow. Afterwards, crystals of quartz and other minerals can form in the void. Agate geodes are rare, however, as the crushing weight of glaciers likely pulverized delicate specimens.

WHERE TO LOOK: Agate geodes tend to be more fragile than most agate varieties, so you'll have better luck in gravel pits near Cloquet and Moose Lake where the agates are buried and less exposed to wind and waves.

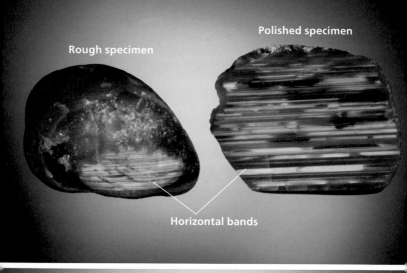

Rough specimen

Polished specimen

Horizontal bands

Polished specimens

Agate, Gravitationally Banded

HARDNESS: 7 **STREAK:** White

Occurrence

ENVIRONMENT: Lakeshore, riverbeds, fields, gravel pits, road cuts

WHAT TO LOOK FOR: Very hard, reddish rounded masses of material containing parallel, horizontal layers or bands within

SIZE: Agates range from pea-sized fragments to fist-sized nodules

COLOR: Multicolored; varies greatly, but banding primarily is red, brown, orange, white and gray

OCCURRENCE: Uncommon

NOTES: In stark contrast to adhesional banded agates, which contain the classic concentric band-within-a-band pattern, gravitationally banded agates contain parallel horizontal bands. Often called water-level agates or onyx, these agates derive their technical name from the fact that only gravity could have produced such straight and level layering. They are theorized to have formed from solutions of silica (quartz compound) that contained excess water; these solutions were therefore too "runny" and unable to adhere to the walls of the vesicle (gas bubble) like in adhesional banded agates. Gravitationally banded agates are scientifically important because they formed due to a different process than all other agate varieties, but they are also popular among collectors and are one of the most desirable agate varieties. One of the most puzzling aspects of these agates can be seen in specimens with horizontal bands that change color and texture along their length. Whatever their appearance, specimens of gravitationally banded agates are some of the easiest of all agate varieties to identify.

WHERE TO LOOK: Gravitationally banded agates occur anywhere agates are found, including lakeshore and riverbeds in northeastern Minnesota and gravel pits near Cloquet and Moose Lake.

Rough specimens

"Moss" growths

Close-up of "moss"

Polished specimen

Small section
of agate
bands

Agate, Moss

HARDNESS: 7 **STREAK:** White

ENVIRONMENT: Lakeshore, riverbeds, fields, gravel pits, road cuts

Occurrence

WHAT TO LOOK FOR: Very hard, red or brown rounded masses of material containing irregular patterns of color and twisting, thread-like inclusions within

SIZE: Agates range from pea-sized fragments to fist-sized nodules

COLOR: Multicolored; varies greatly, but banding is primarily red, brown, orange, white and gray

OCCURRENCE: Common

NOTES: Not all agates have the characteristic banding that agates are known for. Moss agates have a distinctly different appearance and consist of thin, thread-like growths within a mass of irregularly colored chalcedony. So why are moss agates considered agates at all? Technically, they aren't agates, but the definition of an agate has changed many times throughout history and has always been fairly loose. Today, moss agates are agates simply because they are chalcedony and have always been considered agates. However, if you're still skeptical, the occasional presence of concentric banding in Lake Superior moss agates confirms that they formed within the same environment and due to a similar process as traditional agates. The "moss" in moss agates is actually the result of a chemical reaction between iron compounds and the silica (quartz compound) solution from which agates form. But as beautiful and interesting as some Lake Superior moss agates can be, they are common and most are unattractive and undesired by collectors.

WHERE TO LOOK: Moss agates occur anywhere agates are found, including lakeshore in northeastern Minnesota, gravel pits near Cloquet and farm fields throughout the state.

Rough specimens

Inset specimen courtesy
of Jim Cordes

**Paint agate
in basalt**

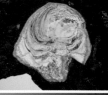

Polished specimens

Agate, Paint

HARDNESS: 7 **STREAK:** White

Occurrence

ENVIRONMENT: Lakeshore, riverbeds, fields, gravel pits, road cuts

WHAT TO LOOK FOR: Very hard, orange or pink rounded masses of material containing opaque, ring-like bands within

SIZE: Agates range from pea-sized fragments to fist-sized nodules

COLOR: Multicolored; varies greatly, but banding is primarily red, pink, brown, orange and tan

OCCURRENCE: Uncommon

NOTES: Paint agates are one of the most popular varieties of Lake Superior agates and derive their name from their opaque coloration, which looks as if it were painted on the stone. Whereas the colored banding in most Lake Superior agates is generally translucent, paint agates exhibit shades of orange, tan and pink that allow no light to shine through them unless the stones are cut very thinly. This unique coloration is a trait that can be found in many types of agates, including adhesional banded, gravitationally banded and sagenitic agates, among others, and it is especially common in any agates that have been very freshly removed from the rock in which they formed. This is because the opaque coloration, often orange due to hematite, is a result of impurities that have not yet been sufficiently exposed to the elements and weathered, a process which reduces the amount of impurities within an agate. This changes both its color and opacity. Lake Superior's shore, especially near Grand Marais, is especially well known for these colorful agates, which are prized by collectors.

WHERE TO LOOK: Many paint agates come out of gravel pits southeast of Duluth, but there are several famous localities along Lake Superior's shoreline, near Grand Marais.

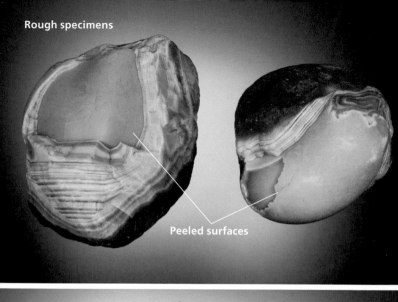

Rough specimens

Peeled surfaces

Rough specimen

Agate, Peeled

HARDNESS: 7 **STREAK:** White

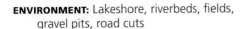

ENVIRONMENT: Lakeshore, riverbeds, fields, gravel pits, road cuts

Occurrence

WHAT TO LOOK FOR: Very hard, reddish rounded masses of material containing ring-like bands within and exhibiting very smooth, waxy exterior surfaces

SIZE: Agates range from pea-sized fragments to fist-sized nodules

COLOR: Multicolored; varies greatly, but banding is primarily red, brown, orange, white and gray

OCCURRENCE: Uncommon

NOTES: Lake Superior agates have not had an easy life. They have existed for more than one billion years and have endured untold amounts of weathering. Different kinds of weathering can affect agates in distinct ways, and peeled agates, often called "peelers" by collectors, are interesting examples of agates that have specifically been altered by cycles of freezing and thawing. As solid as agates seem, they actually contain tiny, microscopic spaces between their bands. Water within these spaces can freeze and expand. Because peeled agates are not very common, we know that freezing an agate normally has little effect. But when an agate experiences this process for thousands of years (along with other forms of weathering), the different layers within an agate can separate and "peel" apart. The result are agates with smooth, waxy surfaces that follow the contours of the banding. The most interesting aspect of these agates is that they give us a look inside the agate at surfaces not normally seen.

WHERE TO LOOK: Because the smooth, peeled surfaces of these agates can be worn and beaten by the waves, they are not often found on lakeshore. Most come out of gravel pits and riverbeds, especially near Duluth and Cloquet.

Rough specimens

Needle-like crystal
inclusions

Radial zeolite formation

Radially arranged needle-like
crystal inclusions

Polished specimens

Agate, Sagenitic

HARDNESS: 7 **STREAK:** White

Occurrence

ENVIRONMENT: Lakeshore, riverbeds, fields, gravel pits, road cuts

WHAT TO LOOK FOR: Very hard, reddish brown rounded masses of material containing bands and fan-shaped growths of needle-like crystals within

SIZE: Agates range from pea-sized fragments to fist-sized nodules

COLOR: Multicolored; varies greatly, but banding is primarily red, brown, orange, white and gray

OCCURRENCE: Uncommon

NOTES: Agates were not the only minerals to grow within vesicles (gas bubbles) in volcanic rocks, nor were they the first. Basalt and rhyolite, the rocks in which agates most commonly develop, formed when lava (molten rock) was forced onto the earth's surface, where it cooled very quickly. As the lava hardened, gases within were trapped as vesicles, providing the void in which agates formed. Water collected in these vesicles, weathering the rock and freeing elements that combined to form new minerals. Zeolites, like thomsonite-(Ca) (page 211), were a result of this process. Many zeolite minerals form as delicate, needle-like crystals arranged into aggregates that radiate from a single point. Sometimes agates formed in vesicles after zeolites had formed (or as they formed), encasing the delicate crystals in chalcedony. Known as sagenitic agates, or simply sagenites, these agates retain the radial zeolite formations and are easily identified and highly collectible. Other needle-like crystals, such as those of goethite (page 131), can produce sagenites as well.

WHERE TO LOOK: Lakeshore, riverbeds and gravel pits in northeastern Minnesota are good places to look.

Rough specimens

Close-up of structure

Polished specimens

Red chalcedony shell

Agate, Skip-an-atom

HARDNESS: 7 **STREAK:** White

Occurrence

ENVIRONMENT: Lakeshore, riverbeds, road cuts

WHAT TO LOOK FOR: Very hard, gray or brown rounded masses of material containing blue or gray opaque crystals within

SIZE: Agates range from pea-sized fragments to fist-sized nodules

COLOR: Multicolored; varies greatly, but primarily brownish or gray on the outside and bluish gray or gray on the inside

OCCURRENCE: Rare

NOTES: While we don't yet know exactly how agates form, we do have some very good theories that account for the many varieties of agates. But Lake Superior is home to one of the strangest and most mysterious agate varieties on earth—skip-an-atom agates. They contain odd segments of opaque, bluish gray quartz with a crackled or fragmented appearance, often arranged into distinct layers. Their peculiar name is derived from an outdated notion that the quartz "skipped an atom" during the agates' formation, resulting in their strange appearance. Though they often exhibit more opaque quartz crystals than agate banding, skip-an-atom agates may not actually be as perplexing as once believed. When heated, quartz and its varieties, including chalcedony, can change and recrystallize into different new forms. When cooled, those new forms can then revert back into quartz. Though the entire process is complicated, it is theorized that skip-an-atom agates were actually regular agates that were heated after formation. Found rarely along Lake Superior's shore, these strange agates are prized by collectors of rare agates, especially when specimens are well banded.

WHERE TO LOOK: Skip-an-atom agates are generally limited to the shores of Lake Superior and nearby rivers.

Rough specimen

Black "smudges" along poorly defined bands

Specimen courtesy of Bradley A. Hansen

Rough specimens

Specimens courtesy of Bradley A. Hansen

Agate, Southern Minnesota

HARDNESS: 7 **STREAK:** White

Occurrence

ENVIRONMENT: Lakeshore, riverbeds, fields, gravel pits, road cuts

WHAT TO LOOK FOR: Very hard, brown, waxy masses of material containing faint layering and dark spots

SIZE: Agates range from pea-sized fragments to fist-sized nodules

COLOR: Multicolored; primarily brown, yellow, gray and black

OCCURRENCE: Rare

NOTES: Generally speaking, most agates found in Minnesota formed in the Lake Superior region. The coldwater agates of southeastern Minnesota are a rare exception and formed as a result of ancient seabeds. Southwestern Minnesota is home to another exception—rare honey-colored masses of faintly banded chalcedony that sometimes turn up in riverbeds. Remarkably similar in color and structure to Montana moss agates from Wyoming and Montana, these "southern Minnesota agates" are certainly an anomaly. Because there are no known agate-producing rocks in that region of the state, these agates were likely deposited in the area by glaciers of past ice ages, but their original source is unknown. The agates themselves exhibit faint banding that is often only visible when backlit; like Montana moss agates they also contain black "smudges," or spots of impurities that exhibit only vague organization. As they were glacially deposited, you'll only be able to find these agates in riverbeds and gravel pits, though their fragmented habit and lack of color make them harder to spot than the Lake Superior agate's reddish brown, well-banded nodules.

WHERE TO LOOK: These rare agates turn up in riverbeds and gravel pits in the southwestern corner of the state.

Whole thunder egg

Cut thunder egg

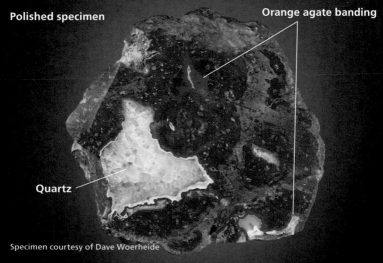

Polished specimen

Orange agate banding

Quartz

Specimen courtesy of Dave Woerheide

Agate, Thunder Egg

HARDNESS: 7 **STREAK:** White

ENVIRONMENT: Riverbeds, gravel pits, road cuts

Occurrence

WHAT TO LOOK FOR: Rough, brown spherical masses containing irregularly shaped regions of ring-like banding within

SIZE: Thunder eggs are typically fist-sized to softball-sized

COLOR: Brown to gray exterior; multicolored interior, including orange, red, brown and white

OCCURRENCE: Rare

NOTES: Thunder eggs are a peculiar variety of agate that can be found near Grand Marais on riverbanks close to Lake Superior. On the outside, a thunder egg simply looks like a rough ball of rock, but its interior contains banded agate patterns. Thunder eggs formed differently than true Lake Superior agates. While true agates formed in vesicles (gas bubbles) in lava, thunder eggs formed within cavities in a type of rock called tuff, which is composed of volcanic ash deposited by explosive volcanic eruptions. However, observant rock hounds will notice that there is no tuff in Minnesota. That's because tuff is soft and weathers easily; when the glaciers scoured the land, the tuff was pulverized, but the hard agates survived. A thunder egg's interior is highly distinctive, with rough, jagged, irregular cavities that are lined with bright orange or red chalcedony banding surrounded by a body of fine-grained brown rock. Nevertheless, their dark, rugged exteriors make them hard to spot on the muddy riverbanks where they are found. When hunting, watch for particularly spherical masses that differ in composition from the basalt and rhyolite you'll likely see a lot of.

WHERE TO LOOK: Though their host rock is long gone, thunder eggs can still be found in riverbeds near Grand Marais, especially close to Lake Superior's shore.

Rough specimens

Tubes within quartz

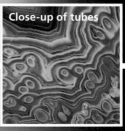

Close-up of tubes

Polished specimens

Agate, Tube

HARDNESS: 7 **STREAK:** White

Occurrence

ENVIRONMENT: Lakeshore, riverbeds, fields, gravel pits, road cuts

WHAT TO LOOK FOR: Very hard, reddish rounded masses of material containing ring-like bands and elongated tube- or needle-like structures within

SIZE: Agates range from pea-sized fragments to fist-sized nodules

COLOR: Multicolored; varies greatly, but banding is primarily red, brown, orange, white and gray

OCCURRENCE: Uncommon

NOTES: Along with sagenitic agates, tube agates are one of the most easily recognizable varieties of Lake Superior agates that contain inclusions of other minerals. Tube agates contain cylindrical structures that developed when the agate formed around zeolites or pre-existing needle-like crystals of minerals such as goethite (page 131). These mineral inclusions are softer than the agate and much more prone to weathering; they often dissolve, leaving a hollow channel at the center of the structure and creating the tube for which these agates are named. Some tube agates still exhibit hollow openings, but many were later filled with additional chalcedony. Hollow or not, the characteristic tubes make these agates distinctive, but they can still be confused with eye agates. When a tube is viewed on its end and does not contain a hollow center, its circular appearance resembles an agate eye, but looking for any signs of elongation or a matching "eye" on the other side of the agate (caused by the tube extending through to the other side) should help.

WHERE TO LOOK: Try the gravel pits near Cloquet and other parts of east-central Minnesota as well as riverbeds in the northeastern corner of the state.

Rough beach-worn specimens

Agate veins

Rhyolite host rock

Polished specimen

Agate, Vein

HARDNESS: 7 **STREAK:** White

ENVIRONMENT: Lakeshore, riverbeds, fields, gravel pits, road cuts

Occurrence

WHAT TO LOOK FOR: Very hard, reddish brown or black elongated masses of material containing ring-like bands within

SIZE: Agates range from pea-sized fragments to fist-sized nodules

COLOR: Multicolored; varies greatly, but banding is primarily red, brown, orange, white and black

OCCURRENCE: Rare

NOTES: There are many types of Lake Superior agates, but nearly every specimen formed in a vesicle (gas bubble) in basalt or rhyolite. Vein agates are the exception to this rule. As their name suggests, vein agates developed in cracks or faults in rocks rather than in round vesicles. Though the resulting agates sometimes exhibit banding that appears very similar to their nodular (round, ball-like) cousins, vein agates can form in any type of rock, including rocks with no vesicles. A particular type of black and white vein agate found in Minnesota is a fine of example of this; it is thought to have originated in iron-rich areas of the state where vesicular rock is not found. Identifying a vein agate once it has weathered from its host rock is difficult, especially if it is rounded and worn by wind and waves, but looking for an elongated banded pattern can help. The finest examples, however, are still in their host rock where the jagged and rough nature of the crack can be easily observed and the unique agate formation appreciated.

WHERE TO LOOK: Vein agates turn up rarely on lakeshore and most come from road cuts or gravel pits, especially in the areas around Duluth and Virginia.

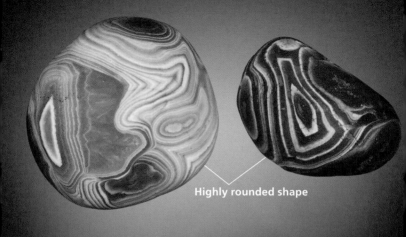

Rough specimens

Highly rounded shape

Rough specimens

Agate, Water-washed

HARDNESS: 7 **STREAK:** White

ENVIRONMENT: Lakeshore, riverbeds, fields, gravel pits, road cuts

Occurrence

WHAT TO LOOK FOR: Very hard, reddish brown, highly rounded and smoothed masses of material exhibiting banding on most or all of its surfaces

SIZE: Agates range from pea-sized fragments to fist-sized nodules

COLOR: Multicolored; varies greatly, but banding is primarily red, brown, orange, white and gray

OCCURRENCE: Uncommon

NOTES: No agate that has been naturally freed from its host rock is without signs of weathering. Most are cracked and worn, and the abuse they endured rarely enhances their appearance. But this isn't the case with water-washed agates. As their name suggests, water-washed agates have been rolled and tumbled in rivers and lakes until their surfaces were rounded and smoothed much more than the average agate. As if sculpted, water-washed agates exhibit no sharp edges, few rough spots and can even be so worn as to appear nearly polished. While their well-shaped nature alone makes them desirable, the most exciting aspect of these agates is that most of their outermost layers have been worn away, exposing the wild, twisting patterns hidden beneath. This makes most water-washed agates beautiful gems with banding visible from all angles, and serious collectors seek the finest examples. Obviously, looking near rivers and lakes is your best bet for finding one.

WHERE TO LOOK: Water-washed agates are primarily found on shores of Lake Superior and inland lakes, but they can occasionally be found in gravel pits near Duluth as well.

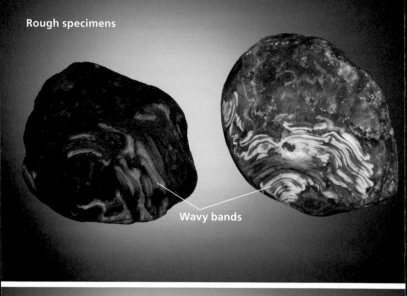

Rough specimens

Wavy bands

Polished specimens

Agate, Whorl

HARDNESS: 7 **STREAK:** White

ENVIRONMENT: Lakeshore, riverbeds, fields, gravel pits, road cuts

Occurrence

WHAT TO LOOK FOR: Very hard, reddish rounded masses of material containing irregular, waving and sweeping bands

SIZE: Agates range from pea-sized fragments to fist-sized nodules

COLOR: Multicolored; varies greatly, but primarily intense reds and whites, also orange, gray and brown

OCCURRENCE: Uncommon

NOTES: Some Lake Superior agates challenge what we think we know about agate formation. Like skip-an-atom agates, whorl agates exhibit strange, almost unexplainable, features. Also called cloud agates or veil agates, whorl agates very often feature intense red and white coloration; in addition, whorls contain odd nonuniform bands that sometimes appear to overlap and have wavy, sweeping curves. This variety of agate has not been studied in detail and we have few theories to account for their growth. One idea is that the whorl banding formed before the rest of the agate. This theory stems from observations of some specimens that contain whorl banding on their outside surfaces but contain regular agate banding deeper within the agate, possibly signifying two generations of chalcedony growth. Whatever their cause, whorls are a unique variety of agate seen almost nowhere else in the world, and most collectors appreciate their curious nature. When the whorl-type banding is subtle, whorl agates can be difficult to identify, but close observation and comparison to the photos shown here should help.

WHERE TO LOOK: Like most Lake Superior agates, whorl agates are found in no particular places, and lakeshore, riverbeds and gravel pits in northeastern Minnesota are best.

Fibrous actinolite crystals
(approximately ⅟₁₆" long)

Hornblende grain
from riverbed (⅛")

Actinolite (green)

Hornblende (greenish black) in granite

⚠ Amphibole group

HARDNESS: 5–6 **STREAK:** White

ENVIRONMENT: Mine dumps, road cuts, lakeshore

Occurrence

WHAT TO LOOK FOR: Dark-colored, fibrous, elongated crystals, masses or grains embedded within rock, particularly granite

SIZE: Most amphibole specimens are thumbnail-sized and smaller

COLOR: Dark yellow to green or brown, gray to black

OCCURRENCE: Common

NOTES: Closely related to the pyroxene group (page 183), the amphibole group of minerals are a family of rock-builders. This means that amphiboles primarily form as small, indistinct grains within rock—in particular, they form in volcanic rocks like granite, gabbro and rhyolite and metamorphic rocks like gneiss and schist. Unfortunately, most amphibole minerals found in Minnesota are difficult to observe and distinguish from other similar minerals. For example, actinolite, an iron-rich amphibole that normally forms as elongated green fibers, is present in greenstone (page 139) and metamorphic rocks, but only as grains that are almost completely indistinguishable from the rest of the rock. Similarly, hornblende, one of the most common minerals on earth, is only easily found in varieties of granite as nondescript black, silky grains or elongated masses. Grunerite and cummingtonite are brown amphiboles notorious in Minnesota's iron mining history. Found in metamorphosed (altered by heat and pressure) iron formations primarily near Biwabik, they are both asbestos, meaning they form as thin, needle-like fibers that can become airborne and are harmful if inhaled. After this discovery, the entire iron-mining process had to be revised.

WHERE TO LOOK: The shore of Lake Superior is great for finding granite containing hornblende, but iron mine dumps near Virginia and Biwabik are better for finding larger masses.

Intergrown analcime crystals

Basalt

Iron-stained crystal

Intergrown crystals

Cluster of many intergrown
fine analcime crystals

Specimen courtesy of Bob Wright

Analcime

HARDNESS: 5–5.5   **STREAK:** White

Occurrence

ENVIRONMENT: Lakeshore, riverbeds, road cuts

WHAT TO LOOK FOR: Small, light-colored, ball-shaped crystals in vesicles, particularly in basalt near Lake Superior

SIZE: Individual analcime crystals range from $\frac{1}{32}$ of an inch wide to pea-sized specimens

COLOR: Colorless to white when pure; more often reddish, orange or brown due to impurities

OCCURRENCE: Rare

NOTES: Analcime is a zeolite mineral, a group which forms in basalt as it is affected by mineral-rich groundwater. There are several zeolite minerals found in the basalt along Minnesota's Lake Superior shoreline, but analcime is one of the few that doesn't form as long, slender, needle-like crystals. Instead, analcime grows as small, faceted, ball-like crystals, often intergrown into large groups. When pure, the colorless or white crystals are glassy and reflect light brightly, making them easy to confuse with crystals of quartz or calcite on first glance. However, those minerals do not share analcime's particular crystal shape or its hardness. When impure and stained with hematite or other minerals, analcime can take on various hues, particularly a brown and reddish orange coloration, but this trait rarely hinders identification. But despite the abundance of basalt and other zeolites, analcime is surprisingly uncommon in Minnesota and is typically only found in the banks of rivers where the rock is highly weathered and decayed.

WHERE TO LOOK: Though derived from basalt, analcime is unexpectedly rare in Minnesota. The rivers and lakeshore near Knife River, Two Harbors and Grand Marais are known to occasionally produce small crystals.

Rough specimens

Dark-colored sample

Rough specimen

Thomsonite-(Ca)

Large glassy feldspar crystals

Specimen courtesy of Bradley A. Hansen

Anorthosite

HARDNESS: ~6–6.5 **STREAK:** N/A

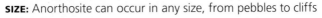
Occurrence

ENVIRONMENT: Lakeshore, riverbeds, road cuts

WHAT TO LOOK FOR: Greenish, light-colored rock made primarily of very coarse, glassy crystals

SIZE: Anorthosite can occur in any size, from pebbles to cliffs

COLOR: Gray to gray-green, bluish and occasionally pale pink

OCCURRENCE: Uncommon

NOTES: Anorthosite is a particularly unique rock in that it consists almost entirely of one mineral—plagioclase feldspar, or, more specifically, labradorite (page 119). Less than ten percent of the rock is comprised of other minerals, though olivine, magnetite and pyroxenes are present. It formed deep within the earth where magma cooled very slowly, allowing large glassy crystals to form within the rock. In this way it can resemble gabbro (page 125), but it should be quickly obvious that anorthosite is much lighter in color and lacks many of the very dark grains found in gabbro, not to mention that anorthosite is far less common. Though there aren't many outcroppings, Split Rock Lighthouse, one of Lake Superior's most famous lighthouses, sits atop an enormous cliff of anorthosite. In 1902, the 3M company was founded with the specific goal of mining Minnesota's anorthosite because they thought it contained corundum, an extremely hard mineral used in abrasives. When they realized their mistake in 1904, it almost broke the fledgling company. And, whether you know it or not, you've already seen anorthosite—it makes up large parts of the moon.

WHERE TO LOOK: One of the best-known outcroppings of anorthosite in Minnesota is a road cut on Highway 61 less than a mile southwest of Silver Bay. Look for enormous masses of light-colored rock embedded within black diabase.

Aragonite crystal (white) on groutite

Inset specimen courtesy
of Bradley A. Hansen

Pseudohexagonal
cross section

Calcite pseudomorphs of aragonite

Specimens courtesy
of Bradley A. Hansen

Aragonite

HARDNESS: 3.5–4 **STREAK:** White

Occurrence

ENVIRONMENT: Mine dumps, fields, road cuts, riverbeds

WHAT TO LOOK FOR: Light-colored crystals, veins or masses that greatly resemble calcite, but are harder

SIZE: Masses of aragonite generally remain smaller than your palm while crystals remain smaller than your thumbnail

COLOR: Colorless to white or gray; yellow to brown when impure

OCCURRENCE: Rare

NOTES: Aragonite is a unique mineral, as its chemical composition is identical to calcite (page 91), but it has an entirely different crystal structure. Aragonite's structure is more compact than calcite's, which distinguishes it as a separate mineral and gives it greater hardness. When well formed, its crystals are elongated and tipped with a point. Crystals are most often found twinned, this means that several crystals are intergrown with each other to form what appears to be a single crystal. Aragonite twins are commonly pseudohexagonal, which means that although a specimen may appear to exhibit a hexagonal, or six-sided, shape, it is actually the result of several blocky crystals that are intergrown and overlap each other. However, because calcite crystals are often hexagonal and occur in the same colors as aragonite—colorless or white when pure, but often brown due to iron staining—it's easy to confuse the two. A hardness test will help, as calcite is much softer. Finally, aragonite is an unstable mineral; in certain environments it actually turns into calcite without changing shape. This creates calcite pseudomorphs, calcite specimens that look like aragonite.

WHERE TO LOOK: There aren't many collecting locations, but mine dumps in the Cuyuna Iron Range, near Crosby, and riverbanks in western Minnesota may yield crystals.

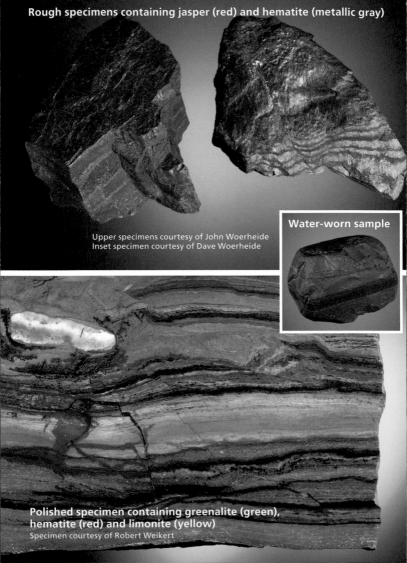

Rough specimens containing jasper (red) and hematite (metallic gray)

Upper specimens courtesy of John Woerheide
Inset specimen courtesy of Dave Woerheide

Water-worn sample

Polished specimen containing greenalite (green),
hematite (red) and limonite (yellow)
Specimen courtesy of Robert Weikert

Banded Iron Formation

HARDNESS: 6–7 **STREAK:** N/A

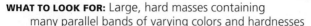

Occurrence

ENVIRONMENT: Mine dumps, riverbeds, road cuts

WHAT TO LOOK FOR: Large, hard masses containing many parallel bands of varying colors and hardnesses

SIZE: Banded iron formations occur in enormous masses, so specimens can range from thumbnail- to boulder-sized

COLOR: Multicolored; varies greatly, but primarily differently colored layers including red, brown, yellow, green and black

OCCURRENCE: Uncommon

NOTES: Minnesota is home to a very unique and scientifically important type of rock called a banded iron formation, or BIF for short. BIFs were formed at the bottom of seas during a period when earth's atmosphere contained far less oxygen than it does today. Cyanobacteria, a kind of blue-green sea algae and one of the first life-forms on earth, played a key role in converting the harsh atmosphere to a more hospitable one. This occurred as a by-product of photosynthesis. In the process, particles of iron dissolved in seawater began to combine with the newly created oxygen and formed minerals like hematite and goethite that precipitated (formed solid particles) and sank. The minerals settled onto beds of mud rich in silica (quartz compound) that formed earlier due to a similar process. Over millions of years, the iron- and silica-rich beds compressed into a beautifully layered rock containing hematite, goethite, limonite, greenalite and many other iron minerals, all interspersed within a body of hard chert and jasper. Many specimens still contain colonies of fossilized cyanobacteria called stromatolites (page 207).

WHERE TO LOOK: Banded iron formations are generally only found in mine dumps near Minnesota's iron ranges, particularly near Virginia, Hibbing, Tower and Crosby.

83

Loose bladed crystal

Crystal cross section

Barite impression in quartz

Intergrown bladed crystals

Calcite crystal

Fine barite crystal cluster

Barite (Baryte)

HARDNESS: 3–3.5   **STREAK:** White

Occurrence

ENVIRONMENT: Road cuts, fields, gravel pits, riverbeds

WHAT TO LOOK FOR: Light-colored, thin, blade-like crystals or masses that feel very heavy for their size

SIZE: Individual crystals are normally no more than an inch or two, but rarely can grow larger. Crystal aggregates or masses can sometimes grow to fist-sized

COLOR: Colorless to white or gray to blue-gray when pure; brown to red or yellow when stained by impurities

OCCURRENCE: Uncommon

NOTES: The world's most abundant barium-bearing mineral is barite. Spelled "barite" in the United States and "baryte" everywhere else, this common mineral is abundant throughout the United States. However, finding Barite in Minnesota is somewhat difficult. Barite is typically found as indistinct light-colored masses in rocks, especially in limestone, clay and other sedimentary rocks like those around the Red River in the western portion of the state, and can be difficult to find as well as identify. There are, however, some telltale signs to look for. Barite has a particularly high specific gravity, which means that even a small specimen will feel very heavy for its size. In addition, while barite has a similar hardness and appearance to calcite, barite will not effervesce, or fizz, in strong vinegar, as calcite will. When well crystallized, such as when found growing in a cavity, barite's bladed crystal shape is highly characteristic and few other Minnesota minerals look quite like it.

WHERE TO LOOK: Masses and crude crystals may be found in western Minnesota, particularly in riverbanks. Cavities in volcanic rocks along Lake Superior's shore have also been known to occasionally produce bladed crystals.

Specimens from Lake Superior

Rough specimen

Vesicles filled with celadonite

Amygdaloidal basalt

Vesicular basalt

Feldspar crystals

Basalt porphyry

Vesicles filled with laumontite

Vesicular basalt

Amygdaloidal basalt

Basalt

HARDNESS: 5–6 **STREAK:** N/A

Occurrence

ENVIRONMENT: All environments

WHAT TO LOOK FOR: Dark, gray to black, very fine-grained rock prominent on lakeshore

SIZE: Basalt can occur in any size, from sand grains to boulders

COLOR: Gray to black, reddish brown to dark brown, greenish

OCCURRENCE: Very common

NOTES: Anyone who has visited Lake Superior is familiar with the dark gray cliffs that frame the lake and cover the shoreline. Most of that rock is basalt, a volcanic rock that forms when lava (molten rock) is spilled onto the earth's surface where it cools and hardens rapidly. This fast solidification process prevents the individual mineral crystals within the rock from growing to a large, visible size; this gives basalt its dark, even-colored and fine-grained appearance. This rapid formation also traps gases within the rock as vesicles (gas bubbles), creating cavities where minerals like zeolites and agates can later form. Basalt with a large number of vesicles is called vesicular basalt, while basalt with most of its vesicles filled by other minerals is called amygdaloidal basalt. Basalt containing rectangular white to orange feldspar crystals that formed before the rest of the rock is called porphyry. Basalt itself is made of an assemblage of dark minerals, including pyroxenes, olivine and plagioclase feldspar in addition to smaller amounts of magnetite and ilmenite, though all are present only as tiny grains. Basalt is so common that it's difficult to confuse it with anything else. Rhyolite (page 193) is lighter in color and harder while diabase (page 115) has small white visible crystals.

WHERE TO LOOK: There is no better place to look than the shores of Lake Superior near Duluth, Two Harbors and Beaver Bay.

Binghamite

Jasper

Quartz

Polished binghamite

Silkstone

Fibrous structure

Binghamite/Silkstone

HARDNESS: ~7 **STREAK:** N/A

ENVIRONMENT: Mine dumps

Occurrence

WHAT TO LOOK FOR: Colorful, fibrous rock containing a mixture of glassy, fibrous and metallic minerals

SIZE: Binghamite and silkstone can be found in a wide range of sizes, from pebbles to boulders

COLOR: Varies greatly; primarily multicolored with white, red, golden yellow and metallic black

OCCURRENCE: Rare

NOTES: Binghamite and silkstone are not distinct minerals but are instead considered varieties of quartz. Both are found only in the Cuyuna Iron Range in central Minnesota, particularly near Crosby, and are formed when silica (quartz compound) interacted with and replaced masses of the iron minerals goethite and hematite while still retaining their fibrous appearance. This resulted in colorful rocks composed primarily of golden yellow fibers that exhibit chatoyance (a band of reflected light) when rotated. In addition, specimens also contain red jasper, white quartz and black hematite. Because both rocks consist mostly of quartz, their high hardness is distinctive in identification as is their very unique appearance. But what is the difference between binghamite and silkstone? Though they formed due to the same process and collectors often don't distinguish one rock from the other and simply label each "binghamite," the traditional definition is that silkstone is more opaque (particularly when polished) and contains coarser fibers that are less organized.

WHERE TO LOOK: The Cuyuna Iron Range is the only locality of binghamite and silkstone, particularly in mine dumps around the towns of Crosby and Ironton and near Rabbit Lake.

Calcite rhombohedrons

Calcite vein in basalt

Massive calcite

Beach-worn calcite

Steep crystal point

Left inset specimen courtesy of Bradley A. Hansen

Right inset specimen courtesy of Christopher Cordes

Crystal in vesicle

Rhombohedral cleavage

Calcite (white) with laumontite (orange)
Specimen courtesy of Jim Cordes

Calcite

HARDNESS: 3 **STREAK:** White

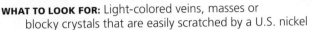

ENVIRONMENT: All environments

Occurrence

WHAT TO LOOK FOR: Light-colored veins, masses or blocky crystals that are easily scratched by a U.S. nickel

SIZE: Individual crystals of calcite are generally no larger than your palm, while masses and veins can be any size

COLOR: Colorless to white, yellow to brown

OCCURRENCE: Very common

NOTES: Calcite, one of the most common minerals on earth, can be found all over Minnesota in one form or another. Due to its abundance and mineralogical importance, all collectors should be able to instantly recognize this mineral. When well crystallized, calcite forms glassy, elongated, six-sided crystals tipped with steep points, but it is far more common as dull white masses filling cracks or vesicles (gas bubbles) in various rocks. Like many minerals, it is colorless or white when pure, but often stained yellow or brown due to iron impurities. Though its modes of occurrence are similar to that of other minerals, identification is very easy. First, its low hardness is often enough to distinguish it from most similar light-colored minerals, such as quartz and aragonite; calcite will be scratched by a U.S. nickel whereas those minerals will not. Second, calcite effervesces (bubbles) in acid, and even a small drop of vinegar will cause calcite to fizz and dissolve, which will distinguish it from barite. Lastly, when carefully broken, calcite will cleave into perfect rhombohedrons (a shape resembling a leaning cube).

WHERE TO LOOK: Lake Superior's shore is an excellent place to find crumbly calcite that easily cleaves into rhombohedrons, while southern Minnesota has produced large, pointed crystals in cavities within limestone and dolostone.

Rough specimens

Rough specimen

Catlinite (Pipestone)

HARDNESS: ~2.5 **STREAK:** N/A

Occurrence

ENVIRONMENT: Fields, road cuts

WHAT TO LOOK FOR: Very soft, reddish, layered rock found in southwestern Minnesota, often alongside hard quartzite

SIZE: As a rock, catlinite can be found in any size, from pebbles to boulders

COLOR: Reddish brown to purple, yellow to cream colored

OCCURRENCE: Rare

NOTES: Catlinite is southern Minnesota's best-known rock. Ancient quarries of the stone, located in Pipestone, were famously visited by American painter George Catlin in 1835, for whom the mineral was later named. Native Americans had been using the sacred quarries for centuries, obtaining the soft, very fine-grained stone for the carving of ceremonial pipes. Catlinite's more informal name, pipestone, derives from this use. Catlinite is actually a variety of argillite, which is mudstone (page 173) consisting of very fine-grained silt and clay that has been partially metamorphosed, or compacted by heat and pressure. The primary minerals within the rock are muscovite (a mica) and pyrophyllite, while the red coloration is caused by iron-rich groundwater that stained the rock. Interestingly, catlinite, one of Minnesota's softest rocks, is found beneath an enormous formation of quartzite (page 189), one of Minnesota's hardest rocks, so the catlinite has been naturally protected from weathering. Identification is simple due to the extreme softness, distinct coloration and association with quartzite.

WHERE TO LOOK: The area around the town of Pipestone is one of the only places in the state to find catlinite, but most samples come from protected Native American land where it is illegal to collect anything.

Beach-worn specimens

Chalcedony in basalt

Waxy luster

Red beach-worn fragments

Chalcedony

HARDNESS: 7 **STREAK:** White

Occurrence

ENVIRONMENT: All environments

WHAT TO LOOK FOR: Hard translucent masses or balls of material that have a waxy appearance and irregular coloration

SIZE: Chalcedony specimens normally are no larger than your palm, but can occasionally be boulder-sized

COLOR: Brown to red, white to yellow, gray; often multicolored

OCCURRENCE: Common

NOTES: Chalcedony is a common microcrystalline variety of quartz. This means that although it is chemically identical to quartz (page 185), its crystals are microscopically small and cannot be seen. As a result, chalcedony lacks the uniform or regular appearance seen in other minerals and instead forms in shapes determined by its surroundings. Chalcedony that forms in vesicles (gas bubbles) takes on a rounded shape, whereas specimens that develop in cracks form in irregular, elongated masses. Chalcedony is best known for being the material from which agates are formed, but not all chalcedony exhibits such exquisite banding. Most specimens are simply masses with mottled coloration caused by impurities of iron minerals. As a variety of quartz, chalcedony is very hard and can only be confused with other quartz-based materials such as chert and jasper. However, while chert and jasper are also microcrystalline quartz, they consist of compact grains of quartz that are not translucent, whereas chalcedony consists of tiny, parallel-oriented quartz fibers, which allow light to shine through. This trait, combined with its waxy appearance, makes it easy to identify.

WHERE TO LOOK: The shore of Lake Superior as well as smaller inland lakes or riverbeds are the best places to hunt for chalcedony.

Quartz

Chalcopyrite

Iridescent coating

Specimen courtesy
of Eric Powers

Chalcopyrite
in gabbro

Chalcopyrite

Pyrite

Specimen courtesy of Dave Woerheide

Chalcopyrite

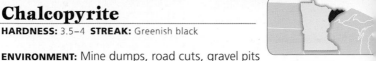

Occurrence

HARDNESS: 3.5–4 **STREAK:** Greenish black

ENVIRONMENT: Mine dumps, road cuts, gravel pits

WHAT TO LOOK FOR: Brittle, soft, brass-yellow masses or veins within rock, often with a blue or pink surface tarnish or yellowish brown stain

SIZE: Chalcopyrite masses can be rarely be fist-sized, but most are pea-sized grains

COLOR: Brass-yellow to golden yellow, metallic brown; sometimes with a blue to purple iridescent surface tarnish

OCCURRENCE: Uncommon

NOTES: Chalcopyrite, a brassy yellow metallic mineral containing copper, iron and sulfur, is typically common elsewhere but difficult to find in Minnesota. Crystals are extremely rare from the state and chalcopyrite is generally only found as small irregular masses embedded within rocks. In this nondescript form, chalcopyrite can be very easily confused with pyrite (page 179), with which chalcopyrite often occurs, and gold (page 133), but a simple hardness test will tell them apart as pyrite is much harder and gold is softer. In addition, pyrite can be found as small cubic crystals, but chalcopyrite doesn't take this form, and gold is very flexible while chalcopyrite is brittle. When weathered, chalcopyrite often develops a colorful surface tarnish that can be easily scratched away to reveal its original color, which is a distinctive trait. In addition, when embedded in rock, weathered chalcopyrite often turns a rusty brown color and stains the surrounding rock with iron. One of the easiest settings in which to spot chalcopyrite is embedded in gabbro, where its color and reflectivity brightly contrast against the dark rock.

WHERE TO LOOK: There aren't many consistent locations. Look for chalcopyrite masses in the gabbro northeast of Duluth.

Beach-worn chert

Coral fossil in chert

Taconite

Rough chert
Specimen courtesy of
Phil Burgess

Fossil snail shell

**Chert (gray) in
siltstone (reddish brown)**

Chert

HARDNESS: 7 **STREAK:** White

Occurrence

ENVIRONMENT: All environments

WHAT TO LOOK FOR: Very hard, opaque, gray masses, often found on beaches as smooth, waxy, naturally polished pebbles or in mine dumps and gravel pits as dull, rough, grainy masses

SIZE: Chert occurs massively and can be found in nearly any size

COLOR: Varies so greatly that color is not a distinguishing feature; often white to gray or black, tan, yellow to brown, reddish

OCCURRENCE: Very common

NOTES: Chert is a very abundant sedimentary rock composed almost entirely of quartz, but it also contains small amounts of other minerals as well as fossil material. It formed when sediments rich in silica (quartz compound) settled to the bottom of ancient sea floors and were compacted. The result is an extremely hard, dense rock. Because of its sedimentary origins, chert can be found in several forms, including magnetite-rich masses called taconite (page 209), rough, ragged growths in limestone and waxy, water-worn pebbles on beaches, all of which may exhibit differently colored layers. Chert is colored yellow or brown by iron impurities and gray to black by organic fossil material. Due to its high quartz content, it shares many of quartz's identifying features, including conchoidal fracture (when struck, circular cracks appear), but that makes it easy to confuse with other forms of quartz like jasper, which is more colorful, chalcedony, which is more translucent, and quartzite, which is grainier and often glassier in appearance.

WHERE TO LOOK: Lake Superior's shore holds waxy, rounded pebbles, the mine dumps of iron ranges yield magnetic taconite, and rivers and gravel pits in central Minnesota produce irregular, rough masses that sometimes contain fossils.

Chlorite lining (green) in basalt vesicle

Calcite

Chlorite (dark green) on greenstone

Chlorite (dark green)

Celadonite (light green)

Chlorite group

HARDNESS: 2–2.5 **STREAK:** Colorless

ENVIRONMENT: Mine dumps, lakeshore, gravel pits, riverbeds, road cuts

WHAT TO LOOK FOR: Soft, dark mineral found lining the insides of vesicles (gas bubbles) in basalt or on the surfaces of agates

SIZE: Individual crystals are tiny and only a few millimeters at their largest, but coatings or masses can be up to fist-sized

COLOR: Commonly light to dark green, occasionally gray to black

OCCURRENCE: Common

NOTES: The chlorite group of minerals, which is closely related to the mica group, consists primarily of clinochlore and chamosite, both of which are present in Minnesota. Telling them apart, however, is virtually impossible without laboratory equipment because they exhibit no appreciable differences from each other. For this reason, nearly all specimens are labelled "chlorite," no matter which mineral they actually are. When well developed, both chamosite and clinochlore are found as tiny, tabular (flat, plate-like), six-sided crystals that line the inner walls of basalt vesicles (gas bubbles). However, it is more likely that you'll find chlorite as a nondescript green lining within the vesicle, often intergrown with other minerals like epidote (page 117) and laumontite (page 155). This is because chlorite forms when the gases that created vesicles begin to interact with the rock, altering the rock's minerals and forming new minerals in the process. Though similar in color to some other minerals, chlorite's low hardness and abundance are key identifiers. Finally, chlorite can also be the result of metamorphism and is the primary mineral in greenstone (page 139).

WHERE TO LOOK: Basalt formations on Lake Superior's shore is your best bet to find vesicles lined with tiny crystals.

Malachite (green)

Chrysocolla (blue)
in basalt

Chrysocolla (greenish blue) on copper

Specimen courtesy of Bradley A. Hansen

Chrysocolla

HARDNESS: 2–4 **STREAK:** White to pale blue

Occurrence

ENVIRONMENT: Mine dumps, riverbeds

WHAT TO LOOK FOR: Soft, pale blue coatings or crusts atop rocks or copper in northeastern Minnesota

SIZE: Coatings of chrysocolla are generally smaller than your palm

COLOR: Bluish green to blue, often very pale

OCCURRENCE: Uncommon

NOTES: A bluish green mineral formed when copper weathers and decays, northern Michigan's copper-rich regions are famous for chrysocolla, but it can be found near Minnesota's Lake Superior shore as well. Its appearance is very distinctive and it is likely the only bright bluish mineral you'll come across in all of Minnesota. And because of the way it forms, it is typically found growing as a coating or cavity-filling mass on or in close association with copper and malachite (page 165), which should eliminate any doubts about its identity. Malachite, which also forms as a result of weathering copper, is typically a vivid green color, but it can occasionally be paler or faintly bluish, making it the only mineral you're likely to confuse with chrysocolla. Their similar hardnesses won't help, so you'll have to rely on other identifying traits. A coating or mass of chrysocolla is often crumbly, dusty and falls apart with little provocation; this occurs because it easily desiccates (dries out) upon exposure to air, which weakens its structure. This trait, along with the fact that chrysocolla exhibits no visible crystal structure, should help distinguish it from malachite, which often shows a fibrous structure.

WHERE TO LOOK: Copper and its related minerals are only easily accessible along Lake Superior, particularly in rivers near Knife River and Beaver Bay.

Kaolinite clay samples

Clay-filled basalt vesicles

Inset specimen courtesy of Jim Cordes

Impure red clay samples

Clay

HARDNESS: 1–2 **STREAK:** N/A

ENVIRONMENT: All environments

Occurrence

WHAT TO LOOK FOR: Very soft masses of material that easily crumble and have a distinctly chalky or earthy feel

SIZE: Individual mineral fragments or crystals in clay are microscopic, but masses of clay can be enormous

COLOR: White to gray, yellow to brown, reddish brown, greenish

OCCURRENCE: Very common

NOTES: Whether or not you're a rock hound, you have no doubt encountered clay, both in its sticky wet form and its soft dry form. But you may not have considered what clay is made of; clay is actually a kind of rock that consists of two primary materials: clay minerals and tiny grains of various materials. Clay minerals are very soft, aluminum-bearing minerals that form as tiny stacks of parallel flat, plate-like crystals that are generally too small to see without a very powerful microscope. These minerals include kaolinite, illite, smectite, montmorillonite and dickite, all of which are present in clays of Minnesota. Very pure clays will consist almost entirely of one or a mixture of these minerals, but most Minnesota clays were influenced by past glacial activity and therefore also include nearly microscopic grains of pulverized rocks, minerals and organic matter. Clay is most frequently associated with bodies of water, such as rivers and lakes, but it can also be found in drier areas. All clays share a key identifying trait—when dry, they are soft and crumbly, but are sticky and soft when wet.

WHERE TO LOOK: Clay can be found in riverbanks anywhere in Minnesota, especially in the northeast, where thick, red, iron-rich clay, deposited by glaciers of past ice ages, underlies much of the landscape near Lake Superior's shore.

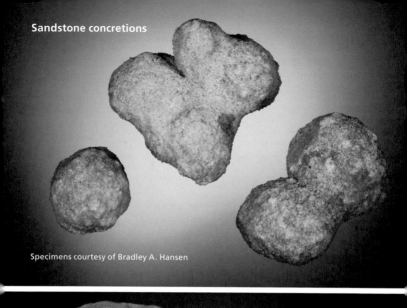

Sandstone concretions

Specimens courtesy of Bradley A. Hansen

Cut iron concretion

Whole iron concretion

Quartz-filled crack

Concretions

HARDNESS: N/A **STREAK:** N/A

ENVIRONMENT: Riverbeds, gravel pits, fields, mine dumps

Occurrence

WHAT TO LOOK FOR: Curiously round rocks, often attached to others, that can almost appear man-made

SIZE: Concretions don't normally form larger than an adult's fist

COLOR: Varies; typically gray to yellow or brown

OCCURRENCE: Uncommon

NOTES: Concretions are a unique kind of rock formation beloved by collectors of all ages. They are spherical masses of rock that are sometimes so round that they may cause amateur collectors to question whether or not they are natural. They are not formed of just one type of rock, but many, including sandstone, clay and even different iron-based minerals, among others, each resulting from a different type of geological environment. Concretions develop when rock particles are cemented around a central point, or nucleus. This nucleus can consist of a range of materials but is typically organic matter, such as a plant particle or an animal shell. As the organic material decays, it releases compounds, such as carbon dioxide, that interact with the surrounding rock, creating new minerals that cement particles of the rock to the nucleus. Sandstone commonly does this, and rough, sandy concretions can be found near rivers in southern Minnesota. Iron concretions are slightly different in that iron-rich groundwater deposited goethite and hematite around a nucleus embedded in soft rock.

WHERE TO LOOK: Sandstone formations in the southern half of the state produce some sandy concretions, especially in riverbanks, while mine dumps in northeastern Minnesota, particularly near Eveleth, rarely produce iron concretions.

Conglomerate

Fossil shark tooth

Conglomerate

Inset specimen courtesy
of Bradley A. Hansen

Water-worn breccia

Conglomerate/Breccia

HARDNESS: N/A **STREAK:** N/A

Occurrence

ENVIRONMENT: All environments

WHAT TO LOOK FOR: Rocks that appear to be made of many smaller rocks that have been cemented together

SIZE: As rocks, conglomerate and breccia can be found in any size, from pebbles to boulders

COLOR: Varies greatly; multicolored

OCCURRENCE: Common

NOTES: Conglomerate and breccia are two types of sedimentary rocks that formed when smaller stones were cemented together by other materials. The stones within them can be any other rock type and give conglomerate and breccia a rough, uneven texture that is easy to recognize. Conglomerate consists of whole, often rounded stones or gravel that is embedded in a finer-grained material, such as sandstone or mudstone, all of which are cemented into a consolidated mass by minerals such as calcite, quartz, or iron-bearing minerals like goethite. Because this process typically takes place in bodies of water, fossils of sea-life, including teeth and shells, can sometimes be found within the rock. Minnesota's Mesabi Iron Range is particularly famous for its 100 million-year-old shark teeth embedded in iron-rich conglomerate. Breccia is similar, but instead of whole stones or pebbles, breccia consists of broken, angular fragments that have been cemented back together. Often these pointed fragments are of the same rock type, signifying that a violent event crushed the original material.

WHERE TO LOOK: While lakeshore and riverbeds contain worn, rounded conglomerate or breccia stones, the Mesabi Iron Range produces fossil-bearing conglomerates, especially near Hibbing, but also near Calumet, Keewatin and Virginia.

Copper on basalt

Copper on basalt

Copper crystal

Chrysocolla (blue)

Weathered sheet copper

All specimens courtesy of Bradley A. Hansen

Copper

HARDNESS: 2.5–3 **STREAK:** Metallic red

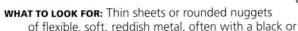

Occurrence

ENVIRONMENT: Riverbeds, lakeshore, gravel pits

WHAT TO LOOK FOR: Thin sheets or rounded nuggets of flexible, soft, reddish metal, often with a black or greenish blue surface tarnish

SIZE: Copper specimens are generally small and no larger than an inch or two in size; masses several feet in size are very rare

COLOR: Copper-red; often with black, green or red tarnish

OCCURRENCE: Uncommon

NOTES: Copper is one of the minerals Lake Superior is famous for, and is far more common in Michigan than it is in Minnesota. Yet the same volcanic activity that created Michigan's "copper country" also formed Minnesota's northern shores, and this same volcanic event caused mineral-rich waters from deep within the earth to rise and deposit copper in cracks and vesicles (gas bubbles) within rocks. Copper is instantly recognizable, as its famous reddish orange color and metallic luster are distinctive and no other Minnesota mineral of a similar appearance has as low a hardness or exhibits such extreme malleability. However, most specimens of copper are found in a weathered state and are coated with a black or red surface tarnish or crusts of green malachite (page 165) and blue chrysocolla (page 103). All of these coatings can easily be scratched off to reveal the copper's true color. Copper typically forms as thin, flexible sheets in between the layers of shale or cracks in basalt, or as nodules in vesicles.

WHERE TO LOOK: Lake Superior's shore rarely yields small rounded nuggets, but rivers near Knife River, Beaver Bay and Grand Marais have produced veins of copper embedded in rock. Gravel pits in northeastern Minnesota may also hold smooth nuggets dropped by glaciers.

Large rough specimen

Cauliflower-like surface structure

Beach-worn fragment

Specimen courtesy of Eric Powers

Cauliflower-like surface structure

Beach-worn specimen

Datolite

HARDNESS: 5–5.5 **STREAK:** White

ENVIRONMENT: Lakeshore, riverbeds

Occurrence

WHAT TO LOOK FOR: Gray or white nodules, often with a cauliflower-like surface texture, that contain hard, porcelain-like interiors

SIZE: Most datolite specimens remain smaller than your fist

COLOR: White to gray

OCCURRENCE: Rare

NOTES: Like copper, datolite is a mineral much more common and famous from Michigan's Keweenaw Peninsula, but it can be found on Minnesota's side of Lake Superior as well. Elsewhere in the world datolite occurs in small, glassy crystals, and only the Lake Superior region produces compact datolite nodules (rounded mineral formations) that formed within pockets in basalt. These specimens are typically found free of their host rock. When whole, the nodules exhibit white, lumpy outer surfaces that often resemble cauliflower. Many specimens, however, were broken open by glaciers and appear as dull, opaque, porcelain-like masses with a chalky texture. Luckily, datolite's hardness is unique to white minerals found on the lakeshore and will be your best identifying trait when a specimen's appearance is indistinct. It should be noted, however, that some specimens are highly weathered and their outer surfaces are slightly softer than unweathered datolite, so a hardness test may initially be misleading. Most specimens are only an inch or two in size, but much rarer specimens measuring several inches have been found.

WHERE TO LOOK: There are not many locations, but Lake Superior's shore near Two Harbors, Beaver Bay and Grand Marais is a good place to start your search.

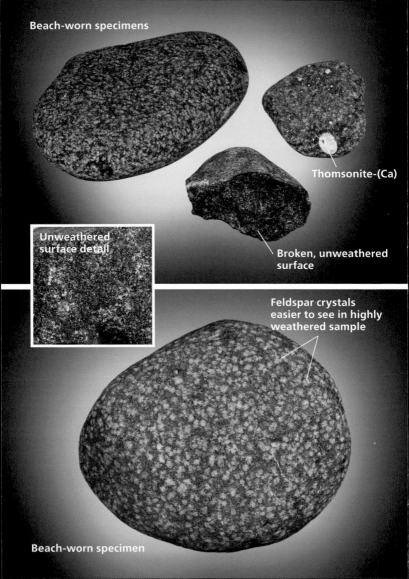

Beach-worn specimens

Thomsonite-(Ca)

Broken, unweathered
surface

Unweathered
surface detail

Feldspar crystals
easier to see in highly
weathered sample

Beach-worn specimen

Diabase

HARDNESS: >5.5 **STREAK:** N/A

Occurrence

ENVIRONMENT: Lakeshore, road cuts, mine dumps, gravel pits

WHAT TO LOOK FOR: Dense, black rock with a medium-grained appearance and "fuzzy" light-colored spots

SIZE: As a rock, diabase can be found in any size, from pebbles and boulders to entire cliffs

COLOR: Typically dark gray to black; occasionally greenish black to brown

OCCURRENCE: Very common

NOTES: Diabase is a dense, black volcanic rock found along Lake Superior's shore in a wide range of sizes, from round water-worn stones to enormous cliffs. Composed primarily of plagioclase feldspar, pyroxene minerals and olivine, diabase is compositionally identical to both gabbro and basalt. The three rocks formed at different depths in the earth, causing the magma (molten rock) from which they formed to cool at different rates. Basalt cooled very rapidly on the earth's surface, giving it a fine-grained appearance, whereas gabbro cooled slowly deep within the earth, giving it its large-grained crystalline appearance. Diabase, however, cooled somewhere in the middle, developing midsized mineral grains that are small, but still visible with the naked eye. Small light-colored feldspar grains are diabase's most distinguishing feature. Though more visible in water-worn specimens, these feldspar crystals look "fuzzy" or "out-of-focus" and formed before the darker minerals.

WHERE TO LOOK: Diabase is most easily identified and collected on Lake Superior's shoreline where the rock is weathered, which makes the "fuzzy" feldspar crystals easier to see. Silver Cliff, northeast of Two Harbors, is largely diabase.

Vesicle in basalt

Epidote crystal (1/16")

Microcline feldspar (pink)

Unakite

Epidote crystals in basalt vesicle

Epidote-lined basalt vesicle
Specimen courtesy of Jim Cordes

Epidote

HARDNESS: 6–7 **STREAK:** Colorless to gray

ENVIRONMENT: Mine dumps, lakeshore, road cuts

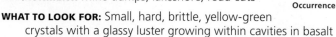

Occurrence

WHAT TO LOOK FOR: Small, hard, brittle, yellow-green crystals with a glassy luster growing within cavities in basalt

SIZE: Individual crystals are rarely more than a few millimeters in size, while crusts or aggregates can measure several inches

COLOR: Yellow-green color is distinctive; also greenish brown

OCCURRENCE: Common

NOTES: Epidote is a rewarding mineral for Minnesota rock hounds to collect because it is easy to identify and features colorful, brightly lustrous and often well-formed crystals. Epidote contains calcium, aluminum and iron, and develops as elongated but very flat and thin crystals with striated (grooved) sides. It frequently grows within vesicles (gas bubbles) in basalt. While its crystals are distinctive in shape and this can help identify specimens, they are often very small—sometimes less than ¼₆₄ of an inch long—making magnification essential. At other times, crystals are not present and epidote instead forms as a thin, lumpy lining inside a vesicle or a coating within a crack in rock. In these situations, you must rely on epidote's most prominent characteristic: its yellow-green color. While the color of most minerals is rarely consistent enough to be the sole identifying trait, epidote is the exception. The pistachio-green coloration is so telling that experienced collectors can often identify epidote at a glance. Unakite, a variety of orange and green granite found on lakeshore, also contains easily identified epidote.

WHERE TO LOOK: The most intact crystals can be found in rough basalt formations near Lake Superior anywhere there is exposed rock. Cracks in granite just north of Virginia on US-53 hold crystals, and unakite can be found near Duluth.

Feldspar crystals (orange) in basalt

Orthoclase in granite

Labradorite grain (⅛") from river

Beach-worn feldspar

Microcline in basalt vesicle

Weathered orthoclase crystal fragments
Specimens courtesy of Bradley A. Hansen

Feldspar group

HARDNESS: 6–6.5 **STREAK:** White

Occurrence

ENVIRONMENT: All environments

WHAT TO LOOK FOR: Very abundant, light-colored blocky crystals found embedded in rocks or growing in cavities

SIZE: Feldspar crystals can occasionally reach several inches in size, but most are thumbnail-sized and smaller

COLOR: White to gray, yellow to orange, brown, greenish

OCCURRENCE: Very common

NOTES: Constituting nearly 60% of the earth's crust, the feldspars are undoubtedly the most common mineral group on the planet. The term "feldspar" itself encompasses over a dozen distinct minerals, several of which are common in Minnesota. The feldspar group is divided into two subgroups: the potassium feldspars, which include orthoclase and microcline, and the plagioclase feldspars, which include labradorite and anorthite. When well developed, all feldspars typically form elongated, blocky, angular crystals in a wide range of colors, but they most commonly occur as grains that make up rocks. The hard, pink regions in granite and the glassy, gray masses in gabbro and anorthosite are particularly prominent examples from Minnesota. When they do develop, freestanding crystals are found in basalt vesicles on Lake Superior's shore and lying loose in gravel pits in the south. Identifying a specimen as a feldspar mineral is easy due to its abundance, high hardness, blocky shapes and light coloration, but distinguishing one feldspar from another can be very difficult without laboratory help.

WHERE TO LOOK: Feldspar minerals can be found everywhere. Masses or loose crystals can be found in any gravel pit or riverbed, and crystals embedded in rocks are easy finds on lakeshore, as are freestanding crystals in basalt vesicles.

Fluorite (purple/green) on basalt

Specimen courtesy of Jim Cordes

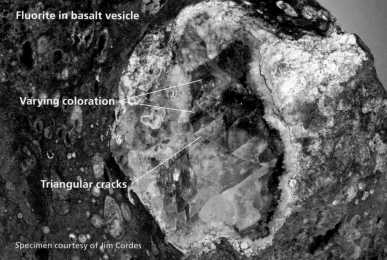

Fluorite in basalt vesicle

Varying coloration

Triangular cracks

Specimen courtesy of Jim Cordes

Fluorite

Occurrence

ENVIRONMENT: Mine dumps, road cuts, fields, riverbeds, gravel pits

WHAT TO LOOK FOR: Soft, glassy, green or purple crystals, masses or veins that often exhibit triangular cracking patterns

SIZE: Fluorite crystals are smaller than your thumbnail, while veins or masses can be several inches in size

COLOR: Colorless to white, pale green, purple; often multicolored

OCCURRENCE: Rare

NOTES: Fluorite is a mineral that is not well known from Minnesota and few collectors from the state have a specimen to call their own. Despite typically being common in many nearby states, this fluorine-bearing mineral is found in very few Minnesota locations, and then only inconsistently. When well formed, fluorite occurs in one of two crystal shapes: cubes or octahedrons (a shape resembling two pyramids placed base-to-base); these two crystal types formed under different temperatures. As with most minerals, however, crystals are rare and fluorite is instead found as glassy masses in shades of purple, green or white, sometimes with layers of all three colors. Crystals often formed within cavities such as cracks in granite or vesicles (gas bubbles) in basalt. But even in its massive form, fluorite is easy to identify, as its hardness is very distinctive. Amethyst (page 187) and calcite (page 91), can look similar, but amethyst is much harder, while calcite is softer.

WHERE TO LOOK: Geodes and vesicles in basalt from rivers and gravel pits around the Grand Marais area very rarely contain purple fluorite, and cracks in granite two miles south of Ely on MN-1 contain tiny purple crystals. Pockets within limestone in southern Minnesota may also yield specimens.

Shark tooth in conglomerate

Clam shell

Left inset specimen courtesy of Phil Burgess

Right inset specimen courtesy of Bradley A. Hansen

Snail shell

Limestone with multiple coral fossils

Coral

Limestone with multiple snail shell fossils

Specimens courtesy of Bradley A. Hansen

Fossils

HARDNESS: N/A **STREAK:** N/A

ENVIRONMENT: All environments

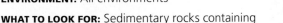

Occurrence

WHAT TO LOOK FOR: Sedimentary rocks containing unique shapes that resemble plants or animal body parts

SIZE: The size of fossils are dependent on the plant or animal that made it; generally palm-sized or smaller

COLOR: Varies greatly; fossils take the color of the surrounding rock, primarily shades of brown, yellow or gray

OCCURRENCE: Rare

NOTES: Always a favorite among collectors, fossils are the remains of once-living plants and animals that have turned to stone. The process of fossilization begins when organic matter, such as an animal bone, is buried in sediment, particularly underwater, where it cannot decay normally. Over the course of millions of years, minerals from the surrounding rock seep into and replace the cells and tissues of the once-living organism, turning it into a mineral formation. As a result, fossils are only found in sedimentary rocks. Minnesota is home to interesting finds for collectors as well as incredibly old and scientifically important fossils. Limestone and chert in southeastern Minnesota are known for containing shells and coral while conglomerate from the Mesabi Iron Range is famous for shark teeth, but these fossils are all very young compared to the 1.9 billion-year-old stromatolites (page 207), the microscopic bacteria fossils found in the Gunflint chert near the Canadian border.

WHERE TO LOOK: Shale along the Mississippi River in the Twin Cities, especially at Lilydale Regional Park, near downtown St. Paul, contains many fossils. Shark teeth are a popular find in conglomerate near Hibbing, and coral can occasionally be found in chert or jasper on Lake Superior's shore.

Rough specimens

Reflective feldspar crystals

Very highly weathered specimen

Beach-worn specimens

Gabbro

HARDNESS: >5.5 **STREAK:** N/A

Occurrence

ENVIRONMENT: Lakeshore, gravel pits, road cuts, mine dumps, riverbeds

WHAT TO LOOK FOR: Dark, very coarsely grained rock containing many embedded jagged, glassy crystals

SIZE: Gabbro can be found in any size, from pebbles to cliffs

COLOR: Multicolored, mottled appearance; primarily greenish gray to black, often with lighter gray sections

OCCURRENCE: Very common

NOTES: Gabbro is a very coarse-grained rock with the same mineral composition as diabase and basalt, but differs in that it formed deep within the earth where molten rock cooled very slowly, allowing the minerals within it to crystallize to a large size. Luckily for rock hounds, this coarse-grained trait makes gabbro one of the easier rocks to identify in Minnesota. Gabbro is a very dark-colored rock, often with a greenish tint, and contains large, thumbnail-sized crystals of plagioclase feldspar that appear as glassy, translucent masses in freshly broken specimens or as dull, lighter-colored shapes in water-worn samples. Often the feldspar masses are so well formed that they exhibit parallel striations (grooves); these derive from their crystal structure and reflect light brightly when viewed at certain angles. Minnesota is home to the Duluth Complex, one of the largest formations of gabbro in the world, and is of significant interest to miners as it contains trace amounts of nickel, gold and platinum, as well as copper, which is evident by occasional embedded masses of chalcopyrite.

WHERE TO LOOK: The Duluth Complex covers much of Minnesota to the northeast of Duluth, but the easiest place to find and identify gabbro is on Lake Superior's shore and riverbeds.

Metamorphic rock

Almandine

Actinolite (green)

Almandine in quartz

Left inset specimen courtesy of Bradley A. Hansen

Garnet grain (1/16") from river sand

Andradite (yellow) with epidote (green)
Specimen courtesy of Jim Cordes

Garnet group

HARDNESS: 6.5–7.5 **STREAK:** Colorless

ENVIRONMENT: Mine dumps, riverbeds, gravel pits

Occurrence

WHAT TO LOOK FOR: Hard, rounded, reddish crystals often embedded in rock or found loose at the bottoms of rivers

SIZE: Garnets can range widely in size, but are normally smaller than your thumbnail and often only millimeters wide

COLOR: Red to brown, pink, rarely yellow

OCCURRENCE: Uncommon

NOTES: Garnet is famous as a gemstone, but the term "garnet" doesn't actually refer to a single mineral; it is the name for a group of closely related minerals. All garnets, including almandine and andradite, the two primary garnet minerals found in Minnesota, typically form as small, ball-like crystals exhibiting many crystal faces. Though their colors can vary, their crystal shape, combined with all garnets' high hardness, is very distinctive, often rendering other tests unnecessary. Garnets can form in several ways, but most are the result of metamorphic activity. When rocks are compressed by heat and pressure, garnets and other similar minerals, like staurolite, are concentrated into pockets. Reddish brown almandine crystals often formed this way and can be found embedded in schist or gneiss as well as alongside fibrous amphibole minerals in iron mine dumps. Tiny yellow andradite crystals are more rare and are found intergrown with epidote within basalt cavities. When weathered out of their host rock, rounded garnets can also be found in river sand.

WHERE TO LOOK: Beautifully weathered red almandines can be found on river bottoms in northeastern Minnesota while larger crystals can occasionally be collected in mine dumps near Crosby. Rare, tiny, yellow andradite crystals are known from cavities in basalt formations near Lake Superior.

Granitic gneiss

Mica schist

Staurolite crystal

Gneiss/Schist

HARDNESS: N/A **STREAK:** N/A

ENVIRONMENT: All environments

Occurrence

WHAT TO LOOK FOR: Hard, layered or banded rock, often containing embedded pockets of garnet or staurolite

SIZE: Gneiss and schist can be found in any size

COLOR: Varies greatly; often multicolored layers in shades of gray, black, brown, white

OCCURRENCE: Common

NOTES: When rocks are subjected to heat and pressure, they undergo great changes in a process called metamorphism. Many rocks that undergo metamorphosis partially melt and their mineral grains are compressed into layers, often transforming them into different minerals in the process. Gneiss (pronounced "nice") and schist are general terms for layered rocks formed by metamorphic activity. Gneiss is traditionally defined as a rock with less than half of its minerals arranged into layers, it therefore still retains much of the original rock's appearance. Gneiss is labelled according to the original rock; for example, granitic gneiss began as granite, and exhibits many of its characteristics. Nearly all of schist's minerals, on the other hand, are arranged into thin, dense, tightly compressed layers, and the minerals have been altered and transformed into different minerals than those in the original rock. Schists are typically labelled according to their dominant mineral; a mica schist, for example, consists primarily of mica minerals.

WHERE TO LOOK: The famous granitic gneiss found along the Minnesota River in Morton is some of the oldest rock on earth at 3.5 billion years old. Black mica schist is particularly prominent near International Falls, as well as in the area south of Little Falls where the schist bears staurolite crystals.

Fragments of fibrous goethite masses

Weathered goethite

Goethite stalactites

Limonite (yellow)

Botryoidal surface

Fibrous banded cross section

Goethite mass

Goethite

HARDNESS: 5–5.5 **STREAK:** Yellow-brown

Occurrence

ENVIRONMENT: Mine dumps, road cuts

WHAT TO LOOK FOR: Black to yellowish brown, metallic mineral exhibiting stalactitic (icicle-like) and/or fibrous structures

SIZE: Masses of goethite can be enormous and several feet in size, but most specimens are fist-sized or smaller

COLOR: Metallic black to brown when fresh; dull yellow to yellow-brown when weathered

OCCURRENCE: Common

NOTES: Pronounced "ger-tite," goethite is one of Minnesota's most important and historic minerals. Goethite, a black, metallic mineral, consists of a combination of iron, oxygen and water; like hematite, it was once one of the primary iron ores mined in the state until the sources were depleted. The modern mining industry has since moved on to taconite (page 209), but specimens of goethite can still be found in mine dumps, particularly in the Cuyuna Iron Range. It can be found in several forms, including botryoidal (grape-like) crusts, stalactitic growths and radial, fibrous masses. Hematite can look very similar and share many of the same growth habits, but it is easy to tell them apart once you know what to look for. When goethite weathers, its surfaces turn a rusty yellow-brown color, whereas hematite turns reddish. The minerals' streak colors exhibit the same key difference. Goethite can also crystallize as tiny, delicate needles in tightly packed groupings, often lining cavities in iron ore, resulting in a "fuzzy," velvety look.

WHERE TO LOOK: Mine dumps in the Cuyuna Iron Range near Crosby and Ironton provide the easiest access to large specimens. Occasionally, rusty, rounded masses are found in gravel pits; some agates contain coarse needles of goethite.

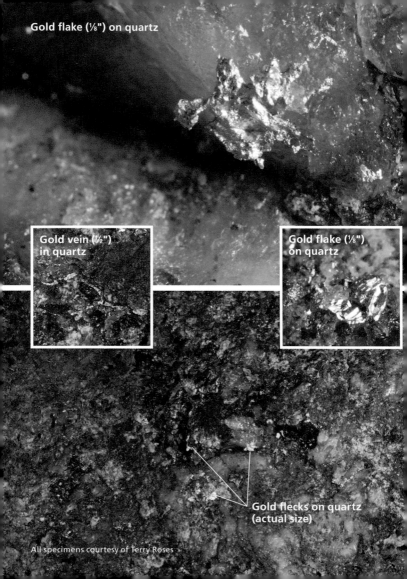

Gold flake (⅛") on quartz

Gold vein (½")
in quartz

Gold flake (⅛")
on quartz

Gold flecks on quartz
(actual size)

All specimens courtesy of Terry Roses

Gold

HARDNESS: 2.5 **STREAK:** Golden yellow

Occurrence

ENVIRONMENT: Riverbeds, road cuts

WHAT TO LOOK FOR: Tiny flecks of bright yellow metallic material, often embedded within quartz or found as small, loose grains at river bottoms

SIZE: Gold specimens are very rarely larger than a pea

COLOR: Metallic yellow

OCCURRENCE: Very rare

NOTES: No mineral has garnered more attention or excitement throughout history than gold. Dozens of U.S. states have had a "gold rush" at some point in their history, in which thousands of prospectors flocked to a potential gold-bearing site, and Minnesota is no exception. A race for gold began in the 1860s and centered around Lake Vermilion and several lakes along the Canadian border, southeast of International Falls. The "Lake Vermilion gold rush," as it is known today, focused on gold-bearing seams of quartz within formations of slate. But because quartz is so hard, freeing the gold was difficult and miners eventually left the area. Today, tiny flecks and thin veins of metallic yellow gold can still be found embedded within layers of quartz around the area, but because the rocks are heavily overgrown, finding anything is extremely difficult. Grains may also be found at river bottoms; this is called placer (pronounced *plasser*) gold and was deposited by weathering. In the unlikely event that you think you've found gold, check its hardness and malleability. If a copper coin can't scratch it, and it's brittle instead of malleable, you've likely found "fool's gold" (page 179).

WHERE TO LOOK: Rainy Lake, Crane Lake and Lake Vermilion were the famous locations for elusive Minnesota gold, but many of the areas are now protected and collecting is illegal.

Rough granite

Unakite (epidote-rich granite)

Beach-worn granite

Granite

HARDNESS: N/A **STREAK:** N/A

ENVIRONMENT: Lakeshore, gravel pits, road cuts, fields, riverbeds

Occurrence

WHAT TO LOOK FOR: Coarse-grained rock containing grains of many different minerals, each easily seen with the naked eye

SIZE: As a rock, granite can be found in any size

COLOR: Varies greatly; primarily mottled spots of white, gray, black, pink, brown and green

OCCURRENCE: Common

NOTES: Granite is one of the most common rocks in the world and makes up a large percentage of the earth's surface, so it is no surprise that it can be found in several places around Minnesota. Granite is a very coarse-grained rock that formed deep within the earth where magma (molten rock) cooled very slowly. This allowed the minerals within it plenty of time to grow to a large, visible size. In contrast, rhyolite contains the same minerals as granite—quartz, orthoclase feldspar, hornblende and micas—but cooled very quickly on the earth's surface, solidifying the minerals in place before they were able to grow large enough to see. Granite is predominantly light colored due to its high quartz and feldspar content, while the darker minerals are confined to small spots, providing a great example of how many different minerals come together to form a rock. Outcrops of granite are exposed sparingly throughout the state while rounded, weathered stones on lakeshore and in gravel pits were carried here from Canada by glaciers.

WHERE TO LOOK: Lake Superior's shore holds Canadian granite deposited by melting glaciers. The area around St. Cloud and Morton is largely underlain by immense granite formations, and more outcrops can be found south of Ely.

135

Polished banded iron formation

Greenalite-rich
chert

Hematite-rich
chert

Specimen courtesy of Robert Weikert

Hematite-rich chert

Greenalite-rich
chert

Rough cross section of
banded iron formation

Greenalite

HARDNESS: 2.5 **STREAK:** Greenish gray

ENVIRONMENT: Mine dumps

Occurrence

WHAT TO LOOK FOR: Hard green layers in iron-rich rocks that also contain hematite, goethite and limonite

SIZE: Greenalite is found in layers that can be up to several feet long, but typically no more than an inch or two thick

COLOR: Green to yellow-green

OCCURRENCE: Rare

NOTES: Greenalite is one of Minnesota's few type-minerals, which means that greenalite was first discovered and identified as a new mineral in Minnesota. Found in 1903 near Biwabik in the banded iron formations (page 83) of the Mesabi Iron Range, it is a member of the serpentine group, a family of closely related, soft and generally green minerals that largely form as a result of other minerals undergoing chemical changes. But Minnesota's greenalite is unusual. It did not form this way, nor does it seem to be as soft as its serpentine cousins. Because it is part of banded iron formations, greenalite does not take a crystalline form, but occurs in dense masses or layers composed of minuscule grains intermixed within chert (page 99). This gives it a perceived hardness of around 7, even though the tiny greenalite grains are much softer (only 2.5). For this reason, among others, greenalite's exact properties were a mystery for years. Due to its "false" hardness, identification is tricky. Look for greenish layers alongside hematite, jasper and chert in banded iron formations—they may contain greenalite, but limonite can be green as well, and unfortunately there is no way to tell them apart when embedded in chert.

WHERE TO LOOK: Finding greenalite is unlikely, but if you do, it will be as thin layers in banded iron formations near Biwabik.

Rough samples

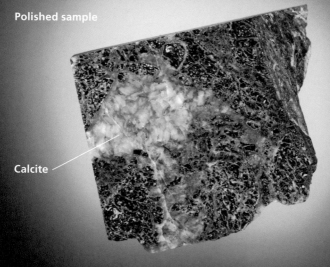

Polished sample

Calcite

Greenstone (Greenschist)

HARDNESS: N/A **STREAK:** N/A

Occurrence

ENVIRONMENT: Road cuts

WHAT TO LOOK FOR: Dense, hard, greenish black rock found in large formations in northeastern Minnesota

SIZE: Greenstone can be found in any size

COLOR: Black to greenish black, bluish green; multicolored

OCCURRENCE: Rare

NOTES: Greenstone is a variety of greenschist, a rock that has undergone such extensive metamorphic changes that the minerals within it have turned into actinolite, chlorite and epidote—all green in color. (Greenstone should not to be confused with the famous "greenstone" gems from Michigan.) Northeastern Minnesota is home to the Ely Greenstone Formation; named for the nearby city of Ely, this formation developed from basalt that originally erupted 2.7 billion years ago onto a sea floor; this is evident by the "pillowed," or rounded, shapes the rock exhibits. For years, dark green, chlorite-rich greenstone was thought to be the oldest rock in the world until further discoveries were made in Canada and Australia. Its dark shades of bluish green are distinctive, and since you're not likely to find greenstone anywhere except the area around Ely, identification is easy. Huge outcroppings and roadcuts of the dense, dark stone can be found to the east and west of town. Few nearby rocks will look quite like it, but if you're having trouble, wet the specimen and look closely for vague signs of parallel layering or streaks of minerals that all seem to go in the same general direction. Also keep an eye out for veins of calcite and small inclusions of brassy pyrite or chalcopyrite.

WHERE TO LOOK: Huge roadside outcroppings are found just west of the city of Ely in northeastern Minnesota.

Groutite crystals lining cavity

Goethite

Bladed crystals

Groutite vein in goethite

Brightly lustrous groutite crystals on quartz

Groutite

HARDNESS: 3.5–4 **STREAK:** Dark brown

Occurrence

ENVIRONMENT: Mine dumps

WHAT TO LOOK FOR: Small, black, brightly metallic curved crystals growing in aggregates atop iron ores such as goethite

SIZE: Individual groutite crystals are typically smaller than a quarter of an inch, while aggregates can be palm-sized

COLOR: Metallic black, brownish black

OCCURRENCE: Very rare

NOTES: Like greenalite, groutite is one of Minnesota's type-minerals, which means that it was first discovered in the state. It is a rare ore of manganese, found only in the manganese-rich iron mines of the Cuyuna Iron Range in central Minnesota, and is closely related to goethite, the iron ore with which it is often found intergrown. As with most of Minnesota's manganese-bearing minerals, it forms black, metallic crystals or masses that are brightly reflective, making it very easy to confuse with minerals such as manganite (page 167) and pyrolusite (page 181). Pyrolusite is harder and often more fibrous in appearance, but distinguishing groutite from manganite is much more difficult. Because they have nearly the same hardness, streak color and identical chemical compositions, you'll have to rely on their only difference: crystal shape. Groutite crystals are bladed or lens-shaped, and when viewed in cross section they typically appear thin with rounded, tapering points on each end, whereas manganite crystals are more blocky and often exhibit deep striations (grooves) on their faces. Groutite is also somewhat rarer than manganite.

WHERE TO LOOK: The Cuyuna Iron Range is the most manganese-rich area of the state and mine dumps in Crow Wing County, particularly near Crosby, are the primary location.

Selenite crystals

Classic selenite crystal shape

The specimen to the left under short-wave ultraviolet light

Gypsum

HARDNESS: 1.5–2   **STREAK:** White

ENVIRONMENT: Fields, riverbeds, road cuts, mine dumps

Occurrence

WHAT TO LOOK FOR: Soft, light-colored masses or angular crystals embedded in clay that are easily scratched by your fingernail

SIZE: Crystals can be palm-sized and sometimes larger, while masses can be several feet in size

COLOR: Colorless to white when pure; often yellow to brown

OCCURRENCE: Common

NOTES: Gypsum is one of the most common sulfur-bearing minerals on earth and has been used as the main ingredient in plaster for millennia. It is also one of the easiest minerals to identify in Minnesota. It primarily forms in beds of sedimentary rocks or clay, often as enormous white masses. A variety of gypsum called selenite is more famous, however; it develops as glassy, transparent crystals that often exhibit a fibrous appearance. Selenite crystals are rectangular and terminate, or end, with oppositely angled points. These crystals are also often twinned, which means that two or more are frequently found intergrown with each other. Depending on their orientation, selenite twins can create heart or fish-tail shapes. While inexperienced collectors may initially see similarities between selenite and calcite or even quartz, selenite's crystal shape is highly distinctive and all forms of gypsum are so soft that they can be scratched by your fingernail. Finally, selenite crystals sometimes exhibit fluorescence under ultraviolet light, glowing in shades of pale blue or greenish yellow.

WHERE TO LOOK: There aren't many locations for fine crystallized specimens, but beds of clay near St. Joseph are known to produce them, as are riverbanks in western Minnesota.

Botryoidal hematite

Botryoidal hematite

Hematite (gray) on quartz (white)

Hematite masses

Red, highly weathered hematite

Hematite

HARDNESS: 5–6 **STREAK:** Reddish brown

Occurrence

ENVIRONMENT: Mine dumps, lakeshore, riverbeds, gravel pits, road cuts

WHAT TO LOOK FOR: Dark gray metallic mineral, often with a reddish surface coloration and fibrous or botryoidal (grape-like) structure

SIZE: Masses of hematite can be any size, up to several feet

COLOR: Steel-gray to black; often with reddish brown surfaces

OCCURRENCE: Common

NOTES: Consisting of a simple combination of iron and oxygen, hematite is the most common iron-bearing mineral on earth and is the primary ore of iron. It has played a major role in Minnesota's history and is common throughout the state. It is typically metallic black and there are a number of ways in which it can form. Botryoidal (grape-like) masses are common from iron-rich areas, such as Minnesota's three iron ranges, and these frequently contain a fibrous structure that is seen in broken specimens. Massive, featureless varieties can be found as well. The reddish stains in minerals, on rocks and in soil are the most common evidence of hematite, and are caused by dusty, fine grains. Note, however, that hematite's modes of occurrence are nearly identical to some of goethite's (page 131). Telling them apart may be difficult when you're just learning their differences, but it's easy with practice. When hematite weathers, it develops a reddish coating, whereas goethite turns a rusty yellow. Their streak colors also reflect this characteristic trait.

WHERE TO LOOK: Mine dumps in the Cuyuna Iron Range, near Crosby and Ironton, yield large specimens, as does the area around the Mesabi Iron Range. Rounded masses can occasionally be found in gravel pits and riverbeds.

Well-formed hematite crystals

Specular hematite

Upper specimen courtesy of Keith Bartel

Left inset specimen courtesy of John Woerheide

Tiny red crystals

Botryoidal "turgite"
Specimen courtesy of John Woerheide

Hematite, varieties

HARDNESS: 5 6 **STREAK:** Reddish brown

Occurrence

ENVIRONMENT: Mine dumps, lakeshore, riverbeds, gravel pits, road cuts

WHAT TO LOOK FOR: Dark gray metallic mineral, often with a reddish surface coloration and fibrous or botryoidal (grape-like) structure

SIZE: Masses of hematite can be any size, up to several feet

COLOR: Steel-gray to black; often with reddish brown surfaces

OCCURRENCE: Uncommon to rare, depending on variety

NOTES: Hematite is so common in Minnesota that it can be found in many distinct varieties. Crystalline hematite, the purest form of hematite as well as the rarest, differs from all other varieties of hematite found in Minnesota in that it exhibits hematite's true crystal shape—tiny, flat, hexagonal (six-sided) plates. Many crystals are so thin that they actually appear blood-red, and this trait gives hematite its name (*hemo* stems from the Greek word for "blood"). These delicate crystals are very rare, however, and casual collectors will likely never find them without considerable research and effort. Micaceous hematite and specular hematite (also called specularite) are also found in Minnesota; they are varieties of hematite that have been subjected to metamorphic conditions. This caused the hematite to recrystallize into a mass of thin, mica-like plates which can make specimens appear "glittery." Finally, a variety called "turgite" can occasionally be found, but it's actually a mixture of both hematite and goethite that displays an iridescent rainbow of color.

WHERE TO LOOK: Mine dumps in the Cuyuna Iron Range, near Crosby and Ironton, rarely produce crystals. Mine dumps in the Vermilion Iron Range, near Tower, contain hematite-stained quartz, specular hematite and turgite.

Ilmenite (metallic black) in gabbro

Ilmenite grains (largest approximately 1/16") from river bottom

Ilmenite

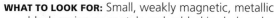

HARDNESS: 5–6 **STREAK:** Brownish black

ENVIRONMENT: Lakeshore, mine dumps, riverbeds

Occurrence

WHAT TO LOOK FOR: Small, weakly magnetic, metallic black grains or crystals embedded in dark rocks or found in black sand

SIZE: Ilmenite specimens remain smaller than your thumbnail, and many are just 1/32 of an inch in size

COLOR: Metallic black; brownish black when highly weathered

OCCURRENCE: Common

NOTES: Ilmenite is common in Minnesota, but only if you know where to look. While other parts of the country yield beautiful, well-formed crystals of ilmenite, Minnesota unfortunately only produces massive varieties that form within gabbro, diabase and basalt as irregularly shaped black metallic grains embedded in the rock. As such, Minnesota's ilmenite is not considered to be very collectible, but it is still interesting considering its titanium content. Identification can be tricky, especially when it is found as tiny grains in rock, but there are a few traits you can watch out for. Ilmenite is black and very frequently brightly metallic, which narrows the possibilities for confusion down to magnetite and hematite. Hematite has a reddish brown streak while ilmenite's is much darker brown. In addition, hematite is not magnetic whereas ilmenite typically exhibits weak magnetism. This differs from magnetite's strong magnetism, so while ilmenite will be attracted to a magnet, it likely won't bond strongly enough to be lifted off a table like magnetite will. Finally, ilmenite shows conchoidal fracturing (when struck, circular cracks appear) and magnetite does not.

WHERE TO LOOK: Well-crystallized specimens are not found in Minnesota, and most specimens are found in gabbro northeast of Duluth or in black sand on shores and in riverbeds. **149**

Beach-worn specimens

Banded jasper

Left inset specimen courtesy of Jodie Blegen

"Jaspilite"

Banded jasper mass
Specimen courtesy of Jim Cordes

Jasper

HARDNESS: 7 **STREAK:** White

ENVIRONMENT: All environments

Occurrence

WHAT TO LOOK FOR: Hard, reddish stones with a waxy feel and appearance; often found alongside hematite

SIZE: Masses of jasper can be found in virtually any size, though specimens are typically palm-sized and smaller

COLOR: Generally red to brown; occasionally yellow to green

OCCURRENCE: Very common

NOTES: Jasper is the name given to colorful varieties of chert (page 99). As such, it is composed of tightly packed microscopic grains of quartz, contributing to its opacity. And like other quartz-based materials, it is very hard and resistant to weathering, exhibiting a waxy texture and appearance when smoothed by wind and waves, but a rough, ragged, dull appearance when freshly exposed. It also displays conchoidal fracturing (when struck, circular cracks appear), as do all forms of quartz. Jasper is most often red or brown in color, which is derived from tiny impurities of hematite, but it can also be yellow to green, though this is rarer. No matter what the color, jasper's great hardness makes it only easily confused with chert and chalcedony. Chalcedony is translucent due to its more organized crystal structure, whereas chert is only found in shades of white, gray and black. "Jaspilite," is a variety of jasper containing gray parallel bands of hematite. Often confused with agates (page 35), jaspilite is more opaque and is a variety of banded iron formation (page 83). "Mary Ellen jasper" contains stromatolites (page 207), an ancient form of ocean life.

WHERE TO LOOK: Lake Superior's shore is the prime collecting site in Minnesota for jasper, but the Mesabi Iron Range, near Hibbing and Virginia, produces banded iron formations.

Beach junk

Tile

Beach glass

Porcelain

Aluminum "blobs"

Beach-worn brick

Driftwood

Beach-worn concrete

Sheet metal

Tar

Slag glass

Junk

HARDNESS: N/A **STREAK:** N/A

ENVIRONMENT: All environments

Occurrence

WHAT TO LOOK FOR: Man-made objects that appear like they "just don't belong" in the environment

SIZE: Varies greatly depending on the size of the junk

COLOR: Varies greatly

OCCURRENCE: Common

NOTES: It never fails: wherever people venture, garbage follows. But while it may seem odd to include man-made junk in a book about rocks and minerals, it can be surprising how often people mistake things like concrete or scraps of metal for minerals. While garbage may normally be easy to identify, certain items are tough enough to withstand weathering, and after water has tumbled and rolled some junk (a piece of glass, for instance) it can look remarkably like a mineral. In fact, collectors often mistake beach glass (small fragments of rounded glass found in beach sand) for quartz. But quartz is harder and less uniform in thickness. Concrete can resemble conglomerate, but the cement holding the rock fragments together is typically harder than the cement in natural conglomerate. Scraps of sheet metal are often large and rusty and don't resemble any natural metals from Minnesota. Shiny, lightweight metal "blobs," while strange and interesting, are merely pieces of aluminum, possibly as mundane as a soda can, that have been rolled and compacted by Lake Superior. Unfortunately, not all junk is accidental. Gravel pits, beloved by rock hounds, often serve as makeshift garbage dumps.

WHERE TO LOOK: Shores of Lake Superior and inland lakes are notorious for water-worn junk, but gravel pits are often used as garbage dumps by senseless people.

Laumontite mass

Calcite

Blocky, fibrous crystals

Laumontite-filled vesicles

Laumontite crystals in basalt vesicle

Laumontite

HARDNESS: 3.5–4 **STREAK:** White

ENVIRONMENT: Lakeshore, riverbeds, road cuts

Occurrence

WHAT TO LOOK FOR: Crumbly, fibrous, orange-colored crystals often intergrown with calcite and found in cavities in basalt

SIZE: Crystals are typically shorter than an inch or two in length

COLOR: Salmon-colored to pink or orange; less commonly white

OCCURRENCE: Common

NOTES: The zeolite group is a family of soft, chemically complex minerals that contain water within their structure. They form primarily as a result of mineral-rich groundwater weathering basalt, providing the material from which new minerals can form. Laumontite is the most common zeolite in Minnesota and can be found in cavities and vesicles (gas bubbles) within the ancient basalt flows of Lake Superior. It is white or light gray when pure, but nearly all the laumontite found in highly weathered basalt is orange or salmon colored due to iron impurities. Sometimes so many laumontite-filled vesicles may be present within a basalt cliff that the rock itself takes on a pinkish hue. Laumontite crystals are elongated fibers arranged into bundles that are very often found alongside calcite, sometimes even penetrating through blocks of the glassy white mineral. Identification is very easy based on visual characteristics alone, but collecting and storing specimens is difficult. Laumontite easily dehydrates, causing it to crumble and turn to dust when exposed to air, and there is little you can do to stop it. It can be confused with thomsonite-(Ca) (page 211), but laumontite is softer.

WHERE TO LOOK: Laumontite is Minnesota's most common zeolite, and easy to find within vesicles in any of Lake Superior's shoreside basalt formations or water-worn pebbles. **155**

Chert

Water-worn
limestone

Rough limestone

Fossil in limestone

Dolostone

Marcasite (metallic) and calcite (white)

Limestone

HARDNESS: 3–4 **STREAK:** N/A

ENVIRONMENT: Fields, gravel pits, road cuts, riverbeds

Occurrence

WHAT TO LOOK FOR: Soft, abundant light-colored rock that is found primarily in flatter areas and may contain fossils

SIZE: Limestone can occur in enormous formations spanning hundreds of miles, though most specimens are palm-sized

COLOR: White to gray, yellow to brown, pink

OCCURRENCE: Very common

NOTES: The presence of large deposits of limestone in Minnesota provides us with unique insight into the state's past. Limestone consists largely of calcite (page 91) and is a common sedimentary rock that forms at the bottom of seas as the remains of tiny aquatic organisms settle and condense into huge, flat beds. When pure, limestone is white or light gray, but Minnesota's limestone is typically yellowish or brown due to impurities of iron minerals. While its light coloration, low hardness, rough and grainy texture, and abundance make it very easy to identify, you can place a drop of strong vinegar on it to be sure. Because limestone consists of over fifty percent calcite, it will effervesce, or fizz in the acidic vinegar. Limestone is also of interest to fossil collectors, as limestone formations, particularly those in southeastern Minnesota, can contain snail and clam shells. Dolostone is a variety of limestone in which dolomite, a close relative to calcite, is the primary constituent, not calcite, and the two rocks cannot be easily distinguished.

WHERE TO LOOK: Limestone and dolostone are particularly common in the entire southeastern corner of Minnesota, near the Mississippi River, as well as in the northwest, particularly along the Red River, bordering North Dakota.

Limonite-coated agate

Red ochre in clay

Limonite on goethite

Limonite in sandstone

Red ochre on hematite

Right inset specimen courtesy of John Woerheide

Goethite core

Limonite mass

Specimen courtesy of John Woerheide

Limonite/Ochre

Occurrence

HARDNESS: 3–5.5 **STREAK:** Yellowish brown/red-brown

ENVIRONMENT: Mine dumps, lakeshore, gravel pits, riverbeds, road cuts

WHAT TO LOOK FOR: Yellowish brown or red masses with a chalky, earthy feel or dusty coatings atop iron-bearing minerals

SIZE: Limonite occurs massively and can be found in any size

COLOR: Limonite is yellow to brown, rust colored; ochre is red to orange, brownish yellow

OCCURRENCE: Very common

NOTES: Limonite and ochre are not particular minerals; rather they are varietal names for masses of unidentified hydrous (water-bearing) iron minerals. Limonite, which is typically yellow-brown or rust colored, consists of grains of various iron-bearing minerals, primarily goethite (page 131), and can be found as masses with a chalky or earthy texture. It forms primarily as a product of iron minerals being weathered and can sometimes contain a core of goethite or hematite, which can contribute a more metallic appearance to a specimen. Distinguishing limonite from other iron ores is easy, however, as limonite has no discernible structure whereas goethite and hematite typically show a fibrous cross section. Limonite is also the primary colorant in yellow soil and can coat other minerals, including agates. Ochre is a varietal name given to red or yellow iron-based pigments and has been used in art for centuries. Red ochre consists of grains of highly weathered hematite, sometimes intermixed within clay; it easily colors your hands red after handling.

WHERE TO LOOK: The Cuyuna Iron Range, near Crosby, the Mesabi Iron Range, near Virginia and Hibbing, and the Vermilion Iron Range, near Tower, are so iron-rich that it would be difficult not to find masses of limonite or ochre.

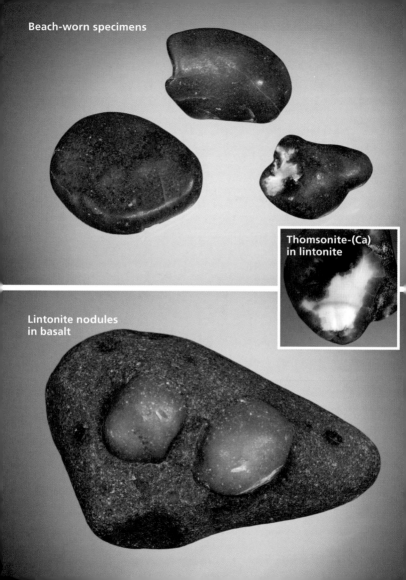

Beach-worn specimens

Thomsonite-(Ca) in lintonite

Lintonite nodules in basalt

Lintonite

HARDNESS: 5–5.5 **STREAK:** White

Occurrence

ENVIRONMENT: Lakeshore

WHAT TO LOOK FOR: Small, rounded, grayish green pebbles on Lake Superior's shoreline

SIZE: Lintonite specimens are most often smaller than your thumbnail

COLOR: Gray-green to blue-green

OCCURRENCE: Rare

NOTES: In the late 1870s, Laura Linton analyzed some unidentified green pebbles found near Grand Marais that she and her colleagues at the University of Minnesota found perplexing. Though the mysterious stones were found to have the same chemical composition as thomsonite, they lacked the structure and optical qualities of that popular zeolite mineral, so Miss Linton felt the pebbles were actually composed of a new, undiscovered mineral. The material was still named in her honor, but we now know that lintonite is not a distinct mineral and is actually a particular massive variety of thomsonite-(Ca) (page 211). As a zeolite, lintonite forms within cavities in basalt, and although true thomsonite-(Ca) can be found intergrown with lintonite, confusing the two is very unlikely. Without the fibrous, needle-like structure and circular patterns that Lake Superior's thomsonite-(Ca) is known for, lintonite shares only its hardness. Often referred to as "jellybeans," the smooth, rounded nodules of dull, gray-green lintonite found on Lake Superior's shore are most easily confused with prehnite, and possibly certain colors of chalcedony, though both are much harder.

WHERE TO LOOK: The shoreline of Lake Superior near Grand Marais and Terrace Point are the best-known locations, but lintonite can rarely be found all along Lake Superior's shore.

Octahedra
magnetite crystal

Magnetite (black)
in gabbro

Magnetite sand
on magnet

Magnetite crystals embedded in hematite

Magnetite

HARDNESS: 5.5–6.5 **STREAK:** Black

Occurrence

ENVIRONMENT: Mine dumps, road cuts, riverbeds, lakeshore

WHAT TO LOOK FOR: Black metallic mineral, often with triangular points, that will attract a magnet

SIZE: Magnetite crystals are generally smaller than your thumbnail, but masses can rarely be several feet in size

COLOR: Iron-black

OCCURRENCE: Common

NOTES: Magnetite, known for its ability to attract a magnet, is one of Minnesota's most important ores of iron. As the primary iron-bearing mineral in taconite, the rock at the center of Minnesota's modern mining industry, magnetite has written itself into the state's history. But despite its abundance and sometimes unexciting appearance, it can still be an interesting and fun mineral for rock hounds to collect. Magnetite is black, metallic and brittle and greatly resembles the similar iron ores hematite and goethite, but those minerals do not share magnetite's magnetism and will not attract a magnet. Magnetite crystals are rare in Minnesota but can be found in mine dumps as small octahedrons (crystals resembling two pyramids placed end-to-end). Most of the time, however, it is found as irregular masses or as tiny grains in rock, such as chert. But the easiest way to find magnetite is by running a magnet through gravel or dark-colored sand. Virtually everything that strongly sticks is magnetite and under magnification you may see small crystals hidden among the grains.

WHERE TO LOOK: The shores of Lake Superior and inland lakes are great places to find magnetic sand, but mine dumps near Tower and Virginia are your only chance for fine crystals.

Radial fibrous malachite growths in basalt

Radial fibrous malachite growths

Malachite

HARDNESS: 3.5–4 **STREAK:** Light green

ENVIRONMENT: Mine dumps

Occurrence

WHAT TO LOOK FOR: Bright green, soft coatings atop copper or other copper-based minerals, such as chrysocolla

SIZE: Malachite occurs as thin coatings or masses in cavities, typically no larger than your thumbnail

COLOR: Dark to light green

OCCURRENCE: Rare

NOTES: Malachite, like chrysocolla (page 103), is the result of copper weathering, breaking down and creating new minerals. In fact, the greenish surface coloration that often develops on copper coins, roofs and artifacts is largely malachite, often with some chrysocolla intergrown with it. Even when well formed, malachite typically does not show much crystal structure, especially in Minnesota. At most, it will form small botryoidal (grape-like) features, but it typically is found as irregular masses or crusts on or in copper-bearing rock. Few other minerals in all of Minnesota share malachite's vivid green coloration—its most characteristic trait—with the exception of chrysocolla, the mineral with which it most often occurs. Chrysocolla, however, is generally more blue in color and is softer, with a chalky, crumbly texture derived from its habit of desiccating, or losing water when exposed to air, a trait malachite does not share. Malachite also often exhibits a radial, fibrous cross section when broken. Unfortunately, malachite is a difficult find. Like much of Minnesota's copper, it forms primarily in the few copper-bearing basalt flows near Lake Superior.

WHERE TO LOOK: The Knife River area is one of the few consistent locations for copper and therefore also contains malachite.

Manganite stalactites

Stalactites

Upper and left inset specimen courtesy of Keith Bartell

Striated crystal

Mass of crude manganite crystals

Manganite

HARDNESS: 4 **STREAK:** Reddish brown to black

Occurrence

ENVIRONMENT: Mine dumps

WHAT TO LOOK FOR: Black, rectangular, striated (grooved) and brightly lustrous crystals lining cavities in iron ores or quartz

SIZE: Most individual manganite crystals are short and under an inch long, but masses can be fist-sized and sometimes larger

COLOR: Metallic gray to iron-black

OCCURRENCE: Rare

NOTES: Manganite is an ore of manganese that formed in the Cuyuna Iron Range's iron ores and can be found infrequently in mine dumps, within cavities in goethite and quartz. Consisting of manganese, oxygen and hydrogen, manganite's chemical composition is identical to that of groutite (page 141), and has a remarkably similar color, metallic luster and streak color; the only discernible difference between them is their crystal shape. Whereas groutite forms rounded, bladed, wedge-like crystals, manganite typically forms elongated, rectangular, blocky crystals with striated (grooved) faces. Sometimes these crystals can be intergrown in large groupings. To make matters more confusing, manganite can also form in radial "sprays" of needle-like crystals; these greatly resembling pyrolusite (page 181). It also forms as stalactites (icicle-like formations). Pyrolusite, however, is harder and has a bluish streak. Finally, one of manganite's most interesting traits is that it can pseudomorph groutite. This means that due to environmental changes, groutite can actually turn into manganite, but it retains the original shape of the groutite crystals. Definitively identifying these specimens is impossible outside of a lab; this is often frustrating for collectors.

WHERE TO LOOK: Try the mine dumps near Crosby and Ironton.

Marcasite mass

Left inset specimen courtesy of Phil Burgess

Right inset specimen courtesy of Christopher Cordes

Marcasite crystals turned into goethite

Marcasite with calcite (white)

Deep striations

Marcasite cockscomb
Specimen courtesy of Christopher Cordes

Marcasite

HARDNESS: 6–6.5 **STREAK:** Dark gray to black

Occurrence

ENVIRONMENT: Mine dumps, gravel pits, road cuts

WHAT TO LOOK FOR: Light-colored, brassy metallic mineral found growing as flat, striated (grooved) pointed crystals or masses

SIZE: Marcasite crystals are rarely larger than your thumbnail, but masses can be fist-sized and larger

COLOR: Light brass-yellow, gray; often with multicolored tarnish

OCCURRENCE: Uncommon

NOTES: Marcasite is an interesting combination of iron and sulfur. It is chemically identical to pyrite (page 179), but is classified as a distinct mineral because of its differing crystal structure, a result of varying conditions during formation. Pyrite is much more common than marcasite, especially in Minnesota, because it forms more easily and requires less specific environmental conditions than marcasite. Although they are both brassy colored and have similar hardnesses, telling the two apart is easy. Marcasite is often deeply striated (grooved), even when massive or broken. When well developed, marcasite's crystals form as flat, tapering points that typically grow side-by-side, giving the appearance of the serrations of a knife. These are called "cockscombs" and are common, particularly in sedimentary rocks like shale, and can later turn into goethite (page 131) if affected by certain conditions. Pyrite, on the other hand, typically forms only as cubic crystals or non-striated masses. Pyrite is also very brass-yellow in color whereas marcasite's metallic coloration is more grayish, often with a multicolored, iridescent surface tarnish. Finally, chalcopyrite can also look very similar, but is much softer.

WHERE TO LOOK: Iron mine dumps near Crosby may yield marcasite, as will cavities in dolostone in southeastern Minnesota.

Muscovite mica sheets

Mica (lustrous gray) in granite

Celadonite nodule in basalt

Right inset specimen courtesy of Jim Cordes

Biotite mica schist

Mica group

Occurrence

HARDNESS: 2.5–3 **STREAK:** Colorless

ENVIRONMENT: Road cuts, gravel pits, riverbeds

WHAT TO LOOK FOR: Shiny, dark-colored minerals that occur in thin, flexible sheets and appear almost metallic

SIZE: Mica crystals are very thin but can be as wide as your palm, though they are generally thumbnail-sized and smaller

COLOR: Commonly colorless to brown, also gray to black, green

OCCURRENCE: Very common

NOTES: Even if you've only been interested in minerals for a short time, you've likely come across paper-thin sheets of a flexible, nearly transparent mineral and wondered what it was. This trait is the hallmark of the micas, a large group of minerals that all form as stacks of parallel sheet-like crystals, not unlike the pages of a book. They are classified as rock-builders, or minerals that primarily contribute to the make-up of rocks. In addition, many micas are brightly reflective, sometimes almost appearing metallic when dark colored. But while a specimen may be easy to identify as a mica, determining which of the many mica minerals it is can be nearly impossible outside of a lab. Muscovite is common and is typically translucent gray or brown in color, while biotite is a name given to micas that are usually darker in color, often black. Celadonite is a dull, blue-green mica often formed within vesicles (gas bubbles) in basalt and can sometimes be found coating agates. Mica schist is a metamorphic rock consisting almost entirely of mica fragments arranged into layers, and catlinite consists largely of tiny muscovite grains.

WHERE TO LOOK: Micas are common in many types of rock, including granite on Lake Superior's shore and mica schist in the north, near International Falls, and in central Minnesota, particularly west of Royalton and south of Little Falls.

Mudstone

Siltstone

Chert layers

Mudstone/Siltstone

HARDNESS: N/A **STREAK:** N/A

ENVIRONMENT: Road cuts, gravel pits, riverbeds, fields, lakeshore

Occurrence

WHAT TO LOOK FOR: Gritty, compact rocks consisting of tiny grains that are smaller than those in sandstone

SIZE: Mudstone and siltstone can both occur in enormous beds, but is often collected as small, palm-sized chunks

COLOR: Varies greatly; typically tan or yellow to brown, also reddish, gray-blue to greenish

OCCURRENCE: Very common

NOTES: Sedimentary rocks are often classified by the size of the tiny grains that constitute them. Sandstone consists of sand-sized particles no larger than $\frac{1}{12}$ of an inch, while siltstone is formed of silt-sized particles typically measuring around $\frac{1}{5,000}$ of an inch. Siltstone is common in Minnesota and can be found as gritty and densely compacted beds of rock, often layered between limestone or other sedimentary rocks. Mudstone is similar but consists of a mixture of assorted sizes of sediments, from silt-sized sediments down to clay-sized, which measure only $\frac{1}{12,500}$ of an inch! Both mudstone and siltstone derive their microscopic grains from the remains of eroded rocks and minerals, and while telling them apart may be difficult without a powerful microscope, they are fairly easy to tell apart from other rock types. Their coloration is often very even and consistent (an indication of their tiny grain size) and they contain no layering. Mudstone or siltstone with easily separated layers is shale (page 197).

WHERE TO LOOK: The Blue Earth River between Mankato and Blue Earth reveals layers of gray siltstone on its banks, and hard, brown masses of siltstone layered with gray chert can occasionally be found on lakeshore near Two Harbors.

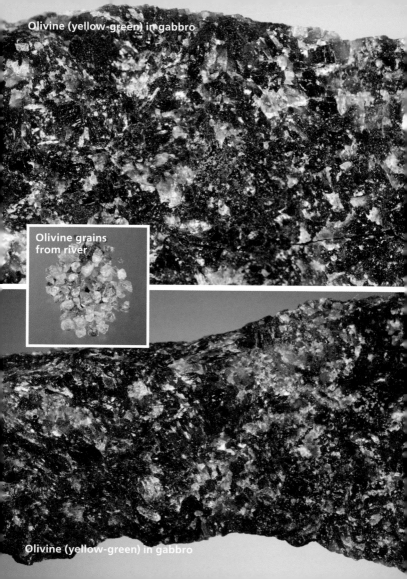

Olivine (yellow-green) in gabbro

Olivine grains from river

Olivine (yellow-green) in gabbro

Olivine group

HARDNESS: 6.5–7   **STREAK:** Colorless

Occurrence

ENVIRONMENT: All environments

WHAT TO LOOK FOR: Very hard, green masses, grains or crystals embedded in rocks, particularly coarse-grained gabbro

SIZE: Olivine occurs in masses smaller than your thumbnail

COLOR: Yellow-green to dark green; sometimes yellow to brown

OCCURRENCE: Common

NOTES: The olivine group consists primarily of two minerals, forsterite and fayalite, though telling the two apart is nearly impossible for amateurs, so most are simply labelled "olivine." Throughout the entire world, olivine crystals are rare, and in Minnesota they are unheard of. Instead, olivine primarily appears as grains or small masses embedded in dark-colored rocks. Basalt contains olivine grains but in most cases they are far too small to be visible without a microscope. Gabbro, on the other hand, is much more coarse-grained, making masses of olivine much easier to identify. Olivine is nearly always translucent green or yellow-green with a glassy luster and no distinct features. Within gabbro, these traits help distinguish olivine from the more prevalent plagioclase feldspar crystals, which are often rectangular, gray and exhibit striations (grooves) along their length. Identification of olivine is easy, as no mineral that contributes to the composition of dark rocks is as hard as olivine. It is possible that inexperienced rock hounds could confuse olivine with epidote, but epidote is more green in color, striated (grooved), and often forms in vesicles (gas bubbles), while olivine does not.

WHERE TO LOOK: Olivine is common within gabbro of the Duluth Complex, which covers much of Minnesota northeast of Duluth. Loose grains may rarely be found on lakeshore.

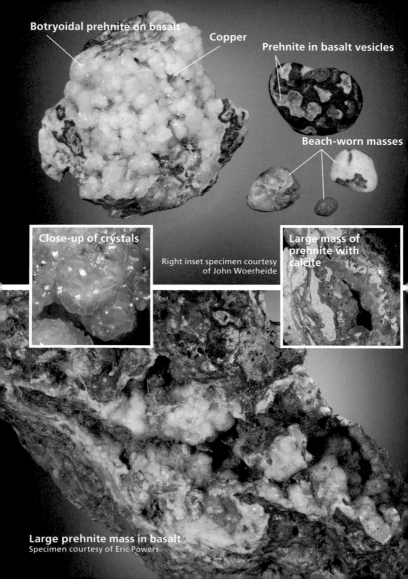

Botryoidal prehnite on basalt

Copper

Prehnite in basalt vesicles

Beach-worn masses

Close-up of crystals

Right inset specimen courtesy of John Woerheide

Large mass of prehnite with calcite

Large prehnite mass in basalt
Specimen courtesy of Eric Powers

Prehnite

HARDNESS: 6–6.5 **STREAK:** White

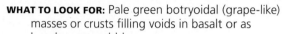
Occurrence

ENVIRONMENT: Lakeshore, riverbeds, gravel pits

WHAT TO LOOK FOR: Pale green botryoidal (grape-like) masses or crusts filling voids in basalt or as beach-worn pebbles

SIZE: Masses of prehnite can be fist-sized, but are generally smaller

COLOR: Light green to gray, white or colorless; rarely pink

OCCURRENCE: Uncommon

NOTES: Prehnite, the first mineral ever named after a person, is a popular Lake Superior collectible found all along its shores. While not common enough to be easily found on every trip to the beach, it certainly isn't rare, and with diligence and a sharp eye you should be able to spot prehnite's characteristic apple-green coloration. Found almost exclusively within basalt, prehnite forms as thin translucent coatings along the inside of cavities, occasionally filling a vesicle (gas bubble) completely if it is small enough. Its surfaces are botryoidal (grape-like) and "lumpy," sometimes with short, crude, bladed ridges along their surfaces. Its pale green color is distinctive, but it can also be gray to white, which can hinder identification. It can also be pink because of tiny copper impurities. The only mineral you could possibly confuse with prehnite is thomsonite-(Ca) (page 211), because prehnite can exhibit a fibrous cross section similar to thomsonite-(Ca) when broken. When in doubt, however, check its hardness, because prehnite is harder than any similar pale-green mineral. Finally, prehnite is often associated with growths of copper and zeolites.

WHERE TO LOOK: Basalt boulders along Knife River are known for large, copper-bearing specimens, but small, beach-worn pebbles are found all along Lake Superior's shore.

177

Pyrite

Upper and right inset specimen courtesy of Dave Woerheide

Pyrite in rock

Pyrite cube (⅛") in greenstone

Striated cubic pyrite crystals

Pyrite

HARDNESS: 6–6.5 **STREAK:** Greenish gray to black

Occurrence

ENVIRONMENT: Mine dumps, gravel pits, riverbeds, road cuts

WHAT TO LOOK FOR: Hard, metallic, brassy yellow masses or striated (grooved) cubic crystals embedded in rock

SIZE: Pyrite crystals are rarely larger than your thumbnail, but masses can be fist-sized and larger

COLOR: Brass-yellow to brown

OCCURRENCE: Common

NOTES: Pyrite is one of the world's most common minerals and is found in virtually every rock type and geological environment, so it is important for all mineral collectors to learn its characteristics. Pyrite has been called "fool's gold" for decades because its coloration is similar to gold's (page 133), but the similarities end there. As a combination of iron and sulfur, brassy yellow pyrite is brittle, whereas gold is very flexible and malleable, and that's not to mention that gold is exceedingly more rare than pyrite. Pyrite does, however, have strong similarities with marcasite (page 169) and chalcopyrite (page 97). When well developed, pyrite forms as perfect cubes and is unmistakable. But more often it is found as irregular rough masses embedded in rock, making it less distinct. Identifying pyrite isn't difficult though, as chalcopyrite is much softer, while marcasite is more gray in color and rarer. Finally, pyrite often rusts as it decays, creating conspicuous brown stains on rocks.

WHERE TO LOOK: Pyrite is found in small quantities in any iron mine dump; try near Tower, Hibbing and Crosby. Cubic crystals are occasionally embedded in metamorphic rocks like gneiss and greenstone in the northeast, and beds of clay, shale or slate all over the state can contain pyrite.

Pyrolusite

Goethite

Pyrolusite vein

Detail of fibrous crystals

Pyrolusite

HARDNESS: 6–6.5 **STREAK:** Black to bluish black

Occurrence

ENVIRONMENT: Mine dumps

WHAT TO LOOK FOR: A black, metallic mineral in fibrous masses or layers in iron-mining areas; often leaves a black sooty dust on your hands after handling

SIZE: Masses and veins of pyrolusite can be up to fist-sized and sometimes larger

COLOR: Black to steel-black, silvery gray; rarely bluish gray

OCCURRENCE: Uncommon

NOTES: Pyrolusite, a metallic mineral composed of manganese and oxygen, is one of the manganese ores produced by the iron mines of the Cuyuna Iron Range in central Minnesota. Frequently occurring as veins or masses of fibrous, black, needle-like crystals arranged into radial groupings, its appearance is quite distinct. But it can be confused with several other minerals, such as goethite (page 131), on which pyrolusite often grows. Goethite often exhibits a fibrous cross section that can resemble that of pyrolusite, but it has a yellow-brown streak and is softer. And though it is very closely related to other manganese minerals like manganite (page 167) and groutite (page 141), you're only likely to confuse pyrolusite with them if found as indistinct masses. A simple hardness test will suffice, as pyrolusite is harder than all other metallic black manganese minerals in Minnesota, and its streak color is also distinctive. But most of the time, you won't even need the streak or hardness tests, as pyrolusite frequently leaves a black, sooty dust on your hands after handling, a strong indication of its presence.

WHERE TO LOOK: The mine dumps around the mining district in Crosby and Ironton are some of the only locations in the state, but beware of privately owned property and railroads.

Augite (black) in gabbro

Blocky cleavage

Augite needles in gabbro

Augite (glassy black) in gabbro

Pyroxene group

HARDNESS: 5–6 **STREAK:** Greenish gray to white

ENVIRONMENT: Lakeshore, gravel pits, mine dumps, riverbeds, road cuts

Occurrence

WHAT TO LOOK FOR: Black to greenish opaque grains or masses embedded in dark-colored rocks

SIZE: Most examples of pyroxene minerals are smaller than your thumbnail, and many are pea-sized and smaller

COLOR: Black to brown; green to greenish gray uncommon

OCCURRENCE: Common to rare, depending on the mineral

NOTES: Like its close relatives, the amphiboles (page 75), the pyroxene group of minerals is a family of rock-builders, or minerals that make up much of the composition of many rocks, particularly dark rocks like basalt and gabbro. Though the pyroxene group encompasses many minerals, only a few are present in Minnesota, and only two of those are easily identified. Augite is the most common and is primarily found as the opaque black and often glassy grains or masses embedded in coarse-grained gabbro. Occasionally augite can be found as crystals in rocks instead of as irregular grains. These crystals have a square, blocky, angular shape; needle-like crystals embedded in rock are much more rare. One of the easiest ways to identify black, nondescript masses of augite in rocks is by its nearly 90-degree cleavage. When carefully broken or weathered, augite will separate at nearly perpendicular angles, forming blocky, square breaks. Diopside, a rare greenish pyroxene, has been found in some iron mines throughout the state, and shares augite's 90-degree cleavage, often forming alongside amphiboles.

WHERE TO LOOK: Gabbro found northeast of Duluth often contains large masses of augite. Dark sand along Lake Superior contains tiny grains of pyroxene minerals as well.

Hematite

Massive quartz

Quartz druse on hematite

Beach-worn sample

Quartz (white) in granite

Quartz-lined vesicle

Iron-stained crystal

Well-formed intergrown quartz crystals

Quartz

HARDNESS: 7 **STREAK:** White

ENVIRONMENT: All environments

Occurrence

WHAT TO LOOK FOR: Light-colored, translucent, very hard and abundant six-sided crystals, masses or veins in rock, or white, water-worn pebbles on beaches

SIZE: Quartz can be found in a large range of sizes, from tiny pea-sized crystals to fist-sized masses

COLOR: Colorless to white, brown to red; uncommonly purple

OCCURRENCE: Very common

NOTES: Quartz is the single most abundant mineral on earth, forming more than 12% of the earth's crust, making it the most important mineral for collectors to study and be able to identify. Consisting entirely of silica, the silicon- and oxygen-bearing material that contributes to hundreds of minerals, quartz forms as distinct hexagonal (six-sided) crystals tipped with a point, often called "rock crystals." Crystals are colorless to white when pure, but are often stained red, brown or yellow due to iron. Formations of quartz druse are common; quartz druse consists of layers of hundreds of tiny intergrown quartz crystals, often lining the insides of cavities, particularly vesicles (gas bubbles) in basalt or cavities in limestone. Massive formless quartz is very common and is often found as veins in cracks or rough masses loose in gravel, but quartz is most common as the most prominent mineral in rocks like granite and chert. Its hardness and crystal shape, if present, are its most diagnostic traits.

WHERE TO LOOK: Quartz is literally found everywhere. Quartz druse can be found in basalt and rhyolite vesicles near Lake Superior, the rock of iron mine dumps near Tower, and cavities in the limestone of southeastern Minnesota. Lakeshore in northern Minnesota harbors much water-worn quartz.

"Cinnamon quartz" on chert

Left inset specimen courtesy of David Gredzens

Beach-worn amethyst

Iron-stained quartz

Amethyst in agate

Quartz, varieties

HARDNESS: 7 **STREAK:** White

ENVIRONMENT: All environments

Occurrence

WHAT TO LOOK FOR: Light-colored, translucent, very hard and abundant six-sided crystals, masses or veins in rock, or white, water-worn pebbles on beaches

SIZE: Quartz can be found in a large range of sizes, from tiny pea-sized crystals to fist-sized masses

COLOR: Red to yellow or brown; purple

OCCURRENCE: Uncommon

NOTES: When a mineral is very abundant and occurs in many different environments, there is a greater potential for it to develop many variations. In Minnesota, quartz is the perfect example of this, and there is no more famous variety of quartz than agates (page 35), a form of microcrystal-line quartz (quartz crystals too small to see). But there are variations of normal quartz as well, including amethyst, which is famous for its purple hues that were caused by iron impurities interacting with natural irradiation. Amethyst can occasionally be found on Lake Superior's shore, particularly near the Canadian border. Only fluorite shares amethyst's color, but fluorite is so much softer that it's difficult to confuse the two. In Minnesota's iron ranges, particularly the Vermilion Range near Ely and Tower, quartz crystals coated with blood-red hematite are sought-after collectibles, as are "cinnamon quartz" specimens stained by iron that have a more orange color. Similarly, yellow-brown quartz is stained by limonite (page 159) but is less desirable than red quartz.

WHERE TO LOOK: Amethyst can be found in the Gunflint area north of Grand Marais as well as on Lake Superior's shore between Two Harbors and the Canadian border. "Cinnamon quartz" and red-stained quartz can be found near Tower.

Rough quartzite

Surface texture detail

Water-worn quartzite

Quartzite

HARDNESS: ~7 **STREAK:** N/A

Occurrence

ENVIRONMENT: Lakeshore, gravel pits, riverbeds, fields, road cuts

WHAT TO LOOK FOR: Very hard, grainy, light-colored rock that shares many of the same traits of quartz

SIZE: Quartzite occurs massively and can be found in any size, from pebbles to boulders

COLOR: White to gray, yellow, brown, occasionally pink or orange

OCCURRENCE: Common

NOTES: Sandstone (page 195) is a sedimentary rock that consists of compacted sand, and sand consists primarily of tiny grains of quartz. When sandstone is subjected to heat and pressure, it compresses, fusing the grains of quartz together and producing a metamorphic rock called quartzite. Quartzite is an extremely hard, tough, weather-resistant rock that consists almost entirely of quartz with some minor amounts of clay, calcite and other minerals that were present in the original sandstone. It is typically white or gray, but is brownish or yellow when stained with iron, and occasionally pink, depending on its impurities. Quartzite greatly resembles chert (page 99), another quartz-based rock, and quartz itself, both in hardness and appearance. However, chert is very opaque whereas thin pieces of quartzite will exhibit translucence, and pure quartz does not have quartzite's often grainy texture or flaky appearance. When all else fails, use magnification to look for signs of graininess.

WHERE TO LOOK: The enormous 1.7 billion-year-old Sioux Quartzite Formation, associated with catlinite, is located in western Minnesota around the towns of Pipestone, Jasper and Jeffers, while the 1.9 billion-year-old Pokegama Quartzite can be found in road cuts near Eveleth and Midway.

Rhodochrosite crystals (orange) in iron ore

Upper and inset specimen
courtesy of Keith Bartel

Rare elongated
crystals

Rhodochrosite vein

Pyrolusite vein
(gray)

Rhodochrosite masses

Rhodochrosite

HARDNESS: 3.5–4 **STREAK:** White

Occurrence

ENVIRONMENT: Mine dumps

WHAT TO LOOK FOR: Soft, pink masses or veins embedded in rock from mine dumps in central Minnesota

SIZE: Masses of rhodochrosite can be several inches in size, but are generally palm-sized or smaller

COLOR: Pale to dark pink, orange; turns brown on exposure to air

OCCURRENCE: Rare

NOTES: Many well-read mineral collectors may know of Montana's or Colorado's world famous rhodochrosite localities, but few know that Minnesota also holds rare specimens of the beautifully colored mineral. A close cousin of calcite, rhodochrosite is a manganese-bearing mineral easily identified by sight alone. Unlike most of the Cuyuna Iron Range's manganese minerals, such as manganite, groutite and pyrolusite, rhodochrosite is not black and metallic but exhibits a glassy, pink or orange coloration. Even when coated in a black manganese dust (produced by weathering) the distinct coloration can still be easily seen on specimens with fresh breaks. Rhombohedral (a shape like a leaning cube) crystals and botryoidal (grape-like) or stalactitic (icicle-like) masses have been found in the past, but these are extremely rare and nearly all specimens found today are masses or veins within fissures in rock. Identification is as simple as noting rhodochrosite's color and hardness, as nothing else in Minnesota will match those traits. If in doubt, however, look for rhombohedral cleavage; when carefully broken, blocks resembling leaning cubes will separate from the specimen.

WHERE TO LOOK: The manganese-rich iron ores of the Cuyuna Iron Range make the mine dumps around Crosby and Ironton the only places to find rhodochrosite in Minnesota. **191**

Rough rhyolite

Beach-worn rhyolite

Vesicular rhyolite

Banded rhyolite

Rhyolite

HARDNESS: 6–6.5 **STREAK:** N/A

Occurrence

ENVIRONMENT: Lakeshore, gravel pits, road cuts, riverbeds

WHAT TO LOOK FOR: Fine-grained, reddish to grayish rock, often with many vesicles (gas bubbles) or colored bands

SIZE: Rhyolite can be found in any size, from pebbles to cliffs

COLOR: Gray, brown to red; sometimes with multicolored bands

OCCURRENCE: Very common

NOTES: When North America was being split open by the Midcontinent Rift 1.1 billion years ago, volcanic lava rose from the depths of the earth to fill the increasing gap. The primary rocks to form at the surface were basalt and rhyolite. Rhyolite formed when lava (molten rock) cooled very rapidly at the earth's surface, causing the minerals within it to freeze in place as tiny grains rather than grow into large, visible crystals. Had rhyolite remained in the earth and cooled very slowly, it would have formed granite, as the minerals in the two rocks are identical and include quartz, potassium feldspars, amphiboles and micas. While rhyolite is typically gray or brown and easy to confuse with basalt, a closer look under magnification will help. Rhyolite lava is more viscous, or thicker, than basalt lava, which means that it holds heat longer. So while rhyolite is still very fine grained, its grains are normally not as small as basalt's, which is an identifying trait. In addition, rhyolite is often reddish and can contain stripes or bands of color caused by the direction of the lava flow, which are also key traits.

WHERE TO LOOK: Lake Superior's shoreline is the primary place to look, especially around Palisade Head and Shovel Point, two massive rock formations made of rhyolite, and near Grand Marais, where brownish gray rhyolite is abundant.

Beach-worn sandstone

Freshly broken sandstone

Greensand

Sandstone with preserved water flow patterns
Specimen courtesy of Jim Cordes

Sandstone

HARDNESS: N/A **STREAK:** N/A

ENVIRONMENT: Lakeshore, riverbeds, gravel pits, road cuts

Occurrence

WHAT TO LOOK FOR: Rocks that occur in layers and have a rough, gritty feel as if made of sand

SIZE: Sandstone can be found in any size, from pebbles to cliffs

COLOR: White to gray, tan to brown are common; red to orange and green are uncommon; often multicolored or banded

OCCURRENCE: Very common

NOTES: Like mudstone and siltstone, sandstone is a sedimentary rock named for the particles that compose it. As its name suggests, sandstone consists of sand that was once deposited in huge beds at the bottoms of seas or lakes. As time passed and the sand was compressed, small amounts of clay, calcite and other soft minerals formed between the grains and cemented them together. The result is a rough rock solid enough to be collected, but loosely compact and crumbly enough that you can easily separate individual grains of sand with your bare hands. Sandstones are often layered, signifying different periods and amounts of settling sand. Usually, sandstone is distinct enough in appearance and texture that you won't confuse it with anything else, but graywacke, a coarse, "dirty" sandstone composed of larger, angular fragments and a large amount of gray clay, can look similar. Finally, greensand is a variety that contains glauconite, a green mica (page 171) that forms at sea bottoms, making the stone green.

WHERE TO LOOK: Enormous formations of sandstone are prevalent around Hinckley, Sandstone and the Twin Cities. Road cuts in and around Red Wing reveal greensand, and cliffs near Grand Marais yield sandstone with preserved water ripples.

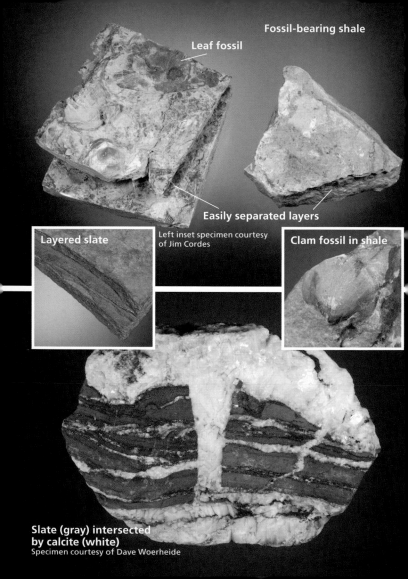

Fossil-bearing shale

Leaf fossil

Easily separated layers

Left inset specimen courtesy of Jim Cordes

Layered slate

Clam fossil in shale

Slate (gray) intersected by calcite (white)
Specimen courtesy of Dave Woerheide

Shale/Slate

HARDNESS: <5.5 **STREAK:** N/A

ENVIRONMENT: Riverbeds, gravel pits, road cuts, fields

Occurrence

WHAT TO LOOK FOR: Fine-grained rocks occurring in layers that can be easily separated by a knife

SIZE: Shale and slate both occur in very large sheets or layers, sometimes many yards, or even miles, wide

COLOR: Shale tan to brown, gray to black; slate gray to black

OCCURRENCE: Shale is common; slate is uncommon

NOTES: Shale is a sedimentary rock composed of compacted, solidified mud that formed at the bottom of very still bodies of water. It consists of microscopic grains of clay minerals, micas and quartz, the remains of weathered and decomposed rocks and minerals that settled into layers during different periods of sedimentation and compaction. As a result, shale is a soft rock and is easily scratched by a knife and comes apart in distinct thin, flat layers. In fact, shale's highly layered nature and low hardness are its most distinguishing features, as non-layered rocks of similar composition to shale are called mudstone (page 173). Because of its aquatic origins, shale often contains fossils, and several shale formations in Minnesota hold snail and clam shells. If shale is subjected to heat and pressure, it compacts and hardens into slate, a black, brittle rock with even thinner layers than shale. Slate is much harder than shale, does not soften when soaked in water, as shale often will, and can occasionally contain pyrite or marcasite in between its layers.

WHERE TO LOOK: Shale can be found along the Mississippi River near downtown St. Paul, as well as in road cuts south of Rochester, where the gray shale contains fossils. Slate can be found in the area around Lake Vermilion.

Dark brown, thin, plate-like siderite crystals

Quartz

Siderite crystals

Black siderite mass

Rhombohedral siderite crystals

Siderite

ENVIRONMENT: Mine dumps, gravel pits

Occurrence

WHAT TO LOOK FOR: Light brown, sometimes iridescent blocky crystals or masses, particularly found in iron mine dumps

SIZE: Siderite crystals remain pea-sized or smaller, while masses can be up to fist-sized and rarely larger

COLOR: Light to dark brown, black; rarely exhibiting iridescence

OCCURRENCE: Uncommon

NOTES: Siderite is a close relative to calcite and rhodochrosite and can be just as collectible as those sought-after minerals. As an iron ore, it is primarily only found in Minnesota's iron ranges, particularly the Cuyuna Iron Range in central Minnesota, and it can exhibit several distinct appearances. When well crystallized, siderite appears as small, glassy, light-brown rhombohedrons, a characteristic shape that looks like a leaning cube. While this crystal shape is shared by rhodochrosite (page 191) and calcite (page 91), confusing these minerals with siderite is unlikely because of rhodochrosite's distinctive pink color and calcite's lower hardness. Crusts of thin, layered, plate-like crystals with an almost metallic iridescent surface coloration are perhaps more collectible than rhombohedrons; these are sometimes found in mine dumps. As with most minerals, siderite is more commonly found as irregular masses, sometimes so dull and indistinct that it can appear to be a rock; you can identify these by looking for any trace of rhombohedral structures.

WHERE TO LOOK: Some of the most beautiful iridescent specimens come from mine dumps near Crosby and Ironton in the Cuyuna Iron Range, but crystals and masses may be found in any mine dumps throughout the state. Irregular earthy masses can occasionally be found in the southeast.

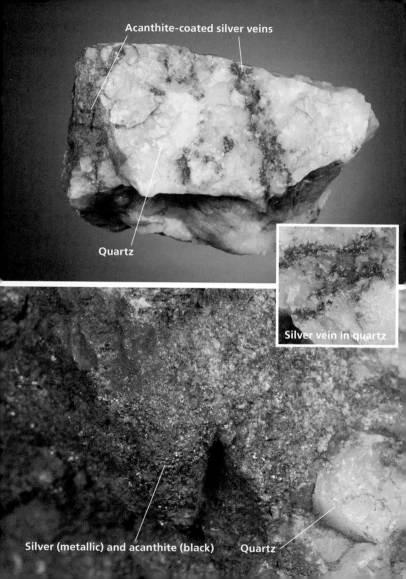

Acanthite-coated silver veins

Quartz

Silver vein in quartz

Silver (metallic) and acanthite (black)

Quartz

Silver

HARDNESS: 2.5–3 **STREAK:** Silvery gray to white

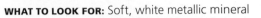

Occurrence

ENVIRONMENT: Mine dumps, riverbeds

WHAT TO LOOK FOR: Soft, white metallic mineral embedded in rock, often with a dark gray surface coating

SIZE: Most silver specimens are thumbnail-sized and smaller

COLOR: Silver-white or gray; dark gray to black when tarnished

OCCURRENCE: Very rare

NOTES: Like gold, silver is an elusive and valuable metal that can rarely be found in Minnesota. As gold and silver form due to identical processes, they are found in the same environments. Therefore, if you're lucky enough to find silver, it will be in one of two places: as tiny flecks or veins embedded in quartz, often alongside chalcopyrite and pyrite, or as tiny rounded grains or nuggets at river bottoms, called placer (pronounced *plasser*) silver. If found in an untarnished state, as water-worn nuggets often are, identification is easy thanks to its distinctive metallic silver coloration, malleability and softness. If embedded in rock, however, silver will likely be tarnished and coated with a dull black or gray patina. This coating is actually another mineral called acanthite, and scratching it removes this tarnish, revealing silver's true coloration. Small, weathered acanthite-coated grains of silver embedded in quartz are often nondescript and featureless, and identification of these specimens will test even experienced rock hounds. In contrast, there is little you could confuse with a shiny placer nugget.

WHERE TO LOOK: Quartz around Rainy Lake, Crane Lake and Lake Vermilion is known to bear silver, but many of the areas are now protected and collecting is illegal. Mine dumps near Tower may also produce specimens embedded in ore and any riverbed in northeastern Minnesota may yield tiny nuggets.

Single staurolite crystals

Staurolite crystal in mica schist

Twinned crystal

Diamond-shaped cross section

All inset and lower specimens courtesy of Dean Montour

Twinned staurolite crystals

Staurolite

HARDNESS: 7–7.5 **STREAK:** White to gray

Occurrence

ENVIRONMENT: Gravel pits, road cuts, riverbeds

WHAT TO LOOK FOR: Hard, dark brown, rectangular crystals with a diamond-shaped cross section, often embedded in dense, shiny black schist

SIZE: Most staurolite crystals are thumbnail-sized

COLOR: Brown, reddish brown, gray

OCCURRENCE: Uncommon

NOTES: Staurolite is a Minnesota collectible that you won't find just anywhere. Virtually the only reliable location is along the Mississippi River in central Minnesota, south of Little Falls, where the river carves its way through a dark mica schist (page 129). Staurolite is embedded in this schist; it formed as a result of metamorphic activity in which sedimentary rocks were heated and compressed, concentrating certain minerals into pockets and transforming them into new minerals in the process. Because of its high-pressure origins, staurolite has a very compact internal crystal structure, which makes it harder than most other Minnesota minerals. Garnets are the only mineral you could confuse with staurolite, but while garnets usually form as round crystals, staurolite always appears as distinctly blocky, elongated, rectangular crystals with a diamond-shaped cross section. Generally brown in color, staurolite crystals can also be twinned, or have other crystals grown through them, sometimes making a perfect cross or "X" shape.

WHERE TO LOOK: Minnesota's best-known staurolite location is near Blanchard Dam just a few miles northwest of Royalton and south of Little Falls. Here, the banks of the Mississippi River hold staurolite and garnet crystals naturally weathered from the schist. Beware of private property, however.

Stilbite crystals in geode

Quartz

Stilbite "wheat-sheaf"

Upper and inset specimen
courtesy of Christopher Cordes

Close-up of crystals

Stilbite

Quartz

Stilbite vein removed from host rock

Stilbite

HARDNESS: 3.5–4 **STREAK:** Colorless

ENVIRONMENT: Lakeshore, riverbeds

Occurrence

WHAT TO LOOK FOR: Delicate sheaf-shaped groupings of pearly orange or pink crystals growing within cavities in basalt

SIZE: Crystal groupings are typically no larger than a thumbnail

COLOR: Pink to orange or brown is common; occasionally gray

OCCURRENCE: Rare

NOTES: Stilbite is one of Lake Superior's rarer members of the zeolite group, a family of chemically complex minerals that are common within cavities in basalt, and to a much lesser extent, rhyolite and anorthosite. Like all zeolites, stilbite primarily forms in vesicles (gas bubbles) in basalt as a result of the rock being weathered by mineral-bearing groundwater, which formed new minerals. Therefore, stilbite can only be found along Lake Superior's shore where basalt cliffs are the prevailing rock formations. Individual crystals are not found in Minnesota; instead stilbite characteristically exhibits striated (grooved), tapering crystal groupings with a pearly luster. Often called "wheat-sheaf" aggregates, due to their resemblance to a bundle of wheat, this shape is stilbite's most diagnostic characteristic and provides all the information you need for identification. Sometimes both ends of crystal groupings will have the sheaf shape, creating what collectors call stilbite "bow-ties." If the classic sheaf shape is not present, however, you'll likely confuse stilbite with laumontite (page 155) due to their similar colors, but laumontite doesn't typically look pearly.

WHERE TO LOOK: Despite the abundance of other zeolites, stilbite is surprisingly rare on Lake Superior's shore. Weathered basalt near Knife River and Grand Marais has produced specimens, but all lakeside basalt could produce stilbite.

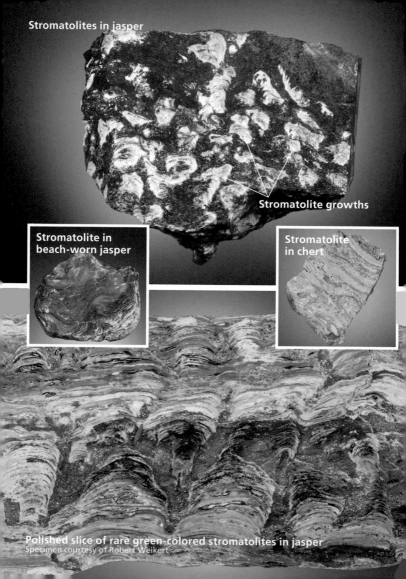

Stromatolites in jasper

Stromatolite growths

Stromatolite in beach-worn jasper

Stromatolite in chert

Polished slice of rare green-colored stromatolites in jasper
Specimen courtesy of Robert Weikert

Stromatolite

HARDNESS: N/A **STREAK:** N/A

Occurrence

ENVIRONMENT: Lakeshore, mine dumps, gravel pits

WHAT TO LOOK FOR: Hard, layered rocks with sweeping, curving shapes within

SIZE: Stromatolite formations embedded in rock can be basket-ball-sized and larger, but many are smaller

COLOR: Multicolored; varies greatly, but primarily bands of gray to black, brown to red and occasionally green

OCCURRENCE: Uncommon

NOTES: In various places around northern Minnesota you can find traces of one of the most important life-forms in earth's history: cyanobacteria. A microscopic blue-green algae that first appeared on earth approximately 3.5 billion years ago, they produced most of the earth's oxygen, turning the harsh, carbon dioxide-rich atmosphere into one more conducive to the evolution of more complex life-forms. They also indirectly led to the formation of thousands of oxygen-bearing minerals. These tiny bacteria clumped together and lived in round colonies in ancient oceans. Their sticky surfaces caught nutrients—and minerals. As minerals accumulated, the colonies grew upward, through the mineral layer, to reach more nutrients. Over the course of millions of years, these colonies, called stromatolites, solidified and were entombed in rock, particularly chert and jasper associated with banded iron formations (page 83). Today, you can find stromatolites as sweeping curved bands within jasper and chert, sometimes with a mushroom-like shape, often containing hematite (page 145). Some people confuse them with agates (page 35), but stromatolites are opaque.

WHERE TO LOOK: Rock outcrops in the Gunflint Formation, near the Canadian border, contain impressive examples.

Rough taconite

Faint layering

Taconite pellet cluster

Loose taconite pellets

Rough taconite
Specimen courtesy of John Woerheide

Taconite

HARDNESS: 6–7 **STREAK:** N/A

ENVIRONMENT: Mine dumps

Occurrence

WHAT TO LOOK FOR: Heavy, hard, black rock that is magnetic and found in iron mining areas, sometimes with colored layers

SIZE: Masses of taconite can be any size, from pebbles to boulders. Taconite pellets are marble-sized

COLOR: Dark gray to black

OCCURRENCE: Uncommon

NOTES: Most books on rocks and minerals don't contain any mention of taconite. That's because the word "taconite," though familiar to Minnesotans, is a mining term first used in northern Minnesota to describe a particular variety of chert containing inclusions of magnetite and some hematite. Taconite, which is frequently associated with banded iron formations (page 83), is a low-grade ore that formed at the bottom of ancient bodies of water when silica, the material of which chert primarily consists, and iron-bearing minerals accumulated into layers. This was caused either by a volcanic process, as in the Vermilion Iron Range, near Tower, or by a sedimentary process in which the two materials settled into immense beds, as in the Mesabi Iron Range, near Virginia, and in the Cuyuna Iron Range, near Crosby. All three iron ranges are locations where taconite can be found as extremely hard, dark gray or black rock with the characteristic magnetism of the magnetite it contains. Taconite pellets, found along railroad tracks, are refined, man-made balls of taconite made for easy transportation of ore. But beware—anyone caught on railroad property is trespassing.

WHERE TO LOOK: Taconite can only be found in Minnesota's iron ranges, particularly in mine dumps in the regions around Crosby, Chisholm, Eveleth, Hibbing, Virginia and Tower.

Rough thomsonite-(Ca) in basalt

Radial fibers

Thomsonite-(Ca) amygdules

Polished specimen

Eye-like formations

Beach-worn nodule

Anorthosite host rock

Thomsonite-(Ca)

Specimen courtesy of Bradley A. Hansen

Thomsonite-(Ca)

HARDNESS: 5–5.5 **STREAK:** White

Occurrence

ENVIRONMENT: Lakeshore, riverbeds

WHAT TO LOOK FOR: Pink or white fibrous masses found as pebbles on the lakeshore or embedded within rock

SIZE: Most thomsonite specimens are smaller than your thumbnail, but are rarely larger

COLOR: White to pink; often multicolored with areas of green

OCCURRENCE: Rare

NOTES: If there's one mineral from Lake Superior's shore that is as popular and collectible as agates, it's thomsonite-(Ca). Like stilbite and laumontite, thomsonite-(Ca) belongs to the zeolite group, a family of chemically complex minerals that form within cavities in weathering basalt and diabase, and rarely anorthosite. When the plagioclase feldspar in these rocks is broken down by mineral-rich groundwater, the resulting solution can produce thomsonite-(Ca). Generally just called "thomsonite" by collectors, the "-(Ca)" in its official name denotes that the variety of thomsonite found on Lake Superior's shore is the calcium-rich type, contrasting with varieties of thomsonite found elsewhere in the world. While finding thomsonite-(Ca) is difficult, identifying it is fairly easy, as it forms nodules (rounded mineral masses) containing radial "sprays" of delicate, white, needle-like crystals, often containing concentric rings of green and pink. It is typically found embedded in basalt vesicles (gas bubbles), but it can be found loose as round pebbles on beaches. It's easy to confuse with prehnite (page 177) and laumontite (page 155), but prehnite is harder, and laumontite is softer.

WHERE TO LOOK: Basalt on beaches and in riverbanks near Grand Marais produces the majority of specimens, while loose pebbles can be found all along Lake Superior's shore.

Intergrown schorl crystals

Specimen courtesy of John Woerheide

Schorl crystal detail

Deep striations

Specimen courtesy of John Woerheide

Tourmaline group

HARDNESS: 7–7.5 **STREAK:** White

Occurrence

ENVIRONMENT: Mine dumps, gravel pits

WHAT TO LOOK FOR: Hard, dark-colored, slender crystals with striated (grooved) sides and a triangular cross section

SIZE: Most tourmaline specimens are thumbnail-sized and smaller

COLOR: Black common; occasionally dark brown

OCCURRENCE: Uncommon

NOTES: The tourmaline group is a family of very chemically complex minerals that form in a manner of ways. In Minnesota, tourmaline typically occurs within metamorphic rocks, and formed in much the same way as garnet or staurolite—through a process that concentrates minerals into pockets within rock as it undergoes heating and pressure. And while there are many tourmaline varieties around the world, only one—schorl—can be found in Minnesota. Schorl is typically opaque, black and glassy, and always appears as long, slender crystals, normally with deeply striated (grooved) sides. Most crystals don't get much more than an inch or two long, but occasionally large intergrown masses will turn up. Schorl is often found still embedded in the schist in which it formed, and this association, combined with its distinct appearance, makes it easily recognizable. If in doubt, however, there are two key traits to look for. If well formed, schorl will exhibit a triangular cross section, often with rounded sides, creating what collectors call a "bulging triangle." This will distinguish schorl from similar amphiboles, as will its greater hardness.

WHERE TO LOOK: Look in places with metamorphic rocks, such as around the lakes near International Falls and the Vermilion Iron Range, near Tower and Ely, where you may find crystals still embedded in the rock. Some sandstones near St. Paul also contain tiny black grains of tourmaline minerals.

GLACIER: Immense sheets and rivers of slow-moving ice, some-times over a mile thick, that scour the earth

GLASSY: A mineral with a reflectivity similar to window glass, also known as "vitreous luster"

GNEISS: A rock that has been metamorphosed so that some of its minerals are aligned in parallel bands

GRANITIC: Pertaining to granite or granite-like rocks

GRANULAR: A texture or appearance of rocks or minerals that consist of grains or particles

HEXAGONAL: A six-sided structure

HOST: A rock or mineral on, or in which, other rocks and minerals occur

HYDROUS: Containing water

ICE AGE: A period of low worldwide temperatures, the last of which ended approximately 10,000 years ago

IGNEOUS ROCK: Rock resulting from the cooling and solidification of molten rock material, such as magma or lava

IMPURITY: A foreign mineral within a host mineral that often changes properties of the host, particularly color

INCLUSION: A mineral that is encased or impressed into a host mineral

IRIDESCENCE: When a mineral exhibits a rainbow-like play of color

LAVA: Molten rock that has reached the earth's surface

LUSTER: The way in which a mineral reflects light off of its surface, described by its intensity

MAGMA: Molten rock that remains deep within the earth

MASSIVE: Mineral specimens found not as individual crystals but rather as solid, compact concentrations; rocks are often described as massive; in geology, "massive" is rarely used in reference to size

MATRIX: The rock in which a mineral forms

METAMORPHIC ROCK: Rock derived from the alteration of existing igneous or sedimentary rock through the forces of heat and pressure

METAMORPHOSED: A rock or mineral that has already undergone metamorphosis

MICA: A large group of minerals that occur as thin flakes arranged into layered aggregates resembling a book

MICACEOUS: Mica-like in nature; said of a mineral consisting of thin sheets

MICROCRYSTALLINE: Crystal structure too small to see with the naked eye

MIDCONTINENT RIFT: A geological event that took place approximately 1.1 billion years ago in which the continent was separating along the present day Lake Superior basin

MINERAL: A naturally occurring chemical compound or native element that solidifies with a definite internal crystal structure

STRIATED: Parallel grooves in the surface of a mineral

STROMATOLITE: A round, layered fossil representing a colony of ancient bacterial algae

TABULAR: A crystal structure in which one dimension is notably shorter than the others, resulting in flat, plate-like shapes

TARNISH: A thin coating on the surface of a metal, often differently colored than the metal itself (see *oxidation*)

TRANSLUCENT: A material that lets some light through

TRANSPARENT: A material that lets enough light through as to be able to see what lies on the other side

TWIN: An intergrowth of two or more crystals

VEIN: A mineral, particularly a metal, that has filled a crack or similar opening in a host rock or mineral

VESICLE/VESICULAR: A cavity created in an igneous rock by a gas bubble trapped when the rock solidified; a rock containing vesicles is said to be vesicular

VUG: A small cavity within a rock or mineral that can become lined with different mineral crystals

WAXY: A mineral with a reflectivity resembling that of wax, such as a candle

ZEOLITE: A group of similar minerals with very complex chemical structures that include elements such as sodium, calcium and aluminum combined with silica and water

Minnesota Rock Shops and Museums

1910 ROCK SHOP
1910 West Highway 61
Grand Marais, MN 55604

AGATE CITY ROCKS AND GIFTS (the authors' store)
721 7th Avenue
Two Harbors, MN 55616
(218) 834-2304

BEAVER BAY ROCK SHOP
1003 Main Street
Beaver Bay, MN 55601
(218) 226-4847

THE ENCHANTED ROCK GARDEN (rock shop)
6445 Lyndale Avenue South
Richfield, MN 55423
(612) 866-1140

MINNESOTA MUSEUM OF MINING
701 West Lake Street
Chisholm, MN 55719
(218) 254-5543

**MOOSE LAKE AGATE AND GEOLOGICAL CENTER
AT MOOSE LAKE STATE PARK** (museum)
4252 County Road 137
Moose Lake, MN 55767
(218) 485-5420

Bibliography and Recommended Reading

Books about Minnesota Minerals

Carlson, Michael. *The Beauty of Banded Agates*. Edina: Fortification Press, 2002.

Lynch, Dan R. and Lynch, Bob. *Agates of Lake Superior.* Cambridge: Adventure Publications, 2011.

Lynch, Bob and Lynch, Dan R. *Lake Superior Rocks & Minerals*. Cambridge: Adventure Publications, 2008.

Marshall, John. *The "Other" Lake Superior Agates*. Beaverton: Llao Rock Publications, 2003.

Ojakangas, Richard W., et al. *Minnesota's Geology*. Minneapolis: University of Minnesota Press, 1982.

Ojakangas, Richard W. *Roadside Geology of Minnesota*. Missoula: Mountain Press Publishing Company, 2009.

Pabian, Roger, et al. *Agates: Treasures of the Earth*. Buffalo: Firefly Books Limited, 2006.

Robinson, Susan. *Is This an Agate?* Hancock: Book Concern Printers, 2001.

Stensaas, Mark "Sparky," *Rock Picker's Guide to Lake Superior's North Shore*. Duluth: Kolath-Stensaas Publishing, 2000.

Zeitner, June Culp. *Midwest Gem, Fossil and Mineral Trails of the Great Lakes States*. Baldwin Park: Gem Guides Book Company, 1999.

General Reading

Bates, Robert L., editor. *Dictionary of Geological Terms, 3rd Edition*. New York: Anchor Books, 1984.

Bonewitz, Ronald Louis. *Smithsonian Rock and Gem*. New York: DK Publishing, 2005.

Chesteman, Charles W. *The Audubon Society Field Guide to North American Rocks and Minerals*. New York: Knopf, 1979.

Johnsen, Ole. *Minerals of the World*. New Jersey: Princeton University Press, 2004.

Mottana, Annibale, et al. *Simon and Schuster's Guide to Rocks and Minerals*. New York: Simon and Schuster, 1978.

Pellant, Chris. *Rocks and Minerals*. New York: Dorling Kindersley Publishing, 2002.

Pough, Frederick H. *Rocks and Minerals*. Boston: Houghton Mifflin, 1988.

Index

About the Authors

Dan R. Lynch has a degree in graphic design with emphasis on photography from the University of Minnesota Duluth. But before his love of the arts came a passion for rocks and minerals, developed during his lifetime growing up in his parents' rock shop in Two Harbors, Minnesota. Combining the two aspects of his life seemed a natural choice and he enjoys researching, writing about, and taking photographs of rocks and minerals. Working with his father, Bob Lynch, a respected veteran of Lake Superior's agate-collecting community, Dan spearheads their series of rock and mineral field guides—definitive guidebooks that help amateurs "decode" the complexities of geology and mineralogy. He also takes special care to ensure that his photographs compliment the text and always represent each rock or mineral exactly as it appears in person. He currently works as a writer and photographer in Madison, Wisconsin, with his beautiful wife, Julie.

Bob Lynch is a lapidary and jeweler living and working in Two Harbors, Minnesota. He has been cutting and polishing rocks and minerals since 1973, when he desired more variation in gemstones for his work with jewelry. When he moved from Douglas, Arizona, to Two Harbors in 1982, his eyes were opened to Lake Superior's entirely new world of minerals. In 1992, Bob and his wife Nancy, whom he taught the art of jewelry making, acquired Agate City Rock Shop, a family business founded by Nancy's grandfather, Art Rafn, in 1962. Since the shop's revitalization, Bob has made a name for himself as a highly acclaimed agate polisher and as an expert resource for curious collectors seeking advice. Now, the two jewelers keep Agate City Rocks and Gifts open year-round and are the leading source for Lake Superior agates, with more on display and for sale than any other shop in the country.

Notes